SECRETS TO
STEWARDING
GOD'S VOICE
IN A NEW ERA

DESTINY IMAGE BOOKS
BY JEREMIAH JOHNSON

The Warrior Bride: Conquering the Five Demonic
Spirits that War Against God's End-Time Church

Prophetic Pioneering: A Call to Build and
Establish God's New Era Wineskins

The Altar: Preparing for the Return of Jesus Christ

Cleansing and Igniting the Prophetic: An Urgent Wake-Up Call

Houses of Glory: Prophetic Strategies for Entering the New Era

Judgment on the House of God: Cleansing and Glory Are Coming

The Power of Consecration: A Prophetic Word to the Church

SECRETS TO
STEWARDING GOD'S VOICE
IN A NEW ERA

THE POWER
AND PRICE OF
INFLUENCE

JEREMIAH JOHNSON

DESTINY IMAGE® PUBLISHERS, INC.

P.O. Box 310, Shippensburg, PA 17257-0310

"Publishing cutting-edge prophetic resources to supernaturally empower the body of Christ"

This book and all other Destiny Image and Destiny Image Fiction books are available at Christian bookstores and distributors worldwide.

For more information on foreign distributors, call 717-532-3040.

Reach us on the Internet: www.destinyimage.com.

ISBN 13 TP: 979-8-8815-0068-9

ISBN 13 eBook: 979-8-8815-0069-6

For Worldwide Distribution, Printed in the U.S.A.

1 2 3 4 5 6 7 8 / 28 27 26 25 24

DEDICATION

To Patricia King, James W. Goll, and Dr. Michael Brown, thank you for your correction, wisdom, and encouragement on my journey. I am indebted to each of you for your prayers, warnings, guidance, and time that you have invested in helping me navigate the influence God has given me. Thank you for modeling integrity, humility, and courage to the global body of Christ. Your love for the truth has radically impacted my life, marriage, and ministry.

CONTENTS

FOREWORD

Y ou have been given a gift. Because of its value, it must be guarded with the greatest of care. Although you had no choice in receiving the gift, you most certainly must choose how you will steward its power, as it will impact every person you come in contact with during your time on earth. And at the end of your days, you will stand before the Giver of this gift and return to Him the reward of His investment.

This treasure you now hold is called influence, and that means you are an influencer.

I don't know about you, but the greatest influencers in my life were not celebrities or people of renown like the so-called "influencers" of this generation. The influencers of my life didn't have large social media or ministry platforms. Social media didn't even exist in their day. And they most certainly didn't use their voices of opinion for cultural effect, political power, or monetary gain.

Unlike the influencers of this generation, the greatest influencers in my life lived simple, uncomplicated lives. They read their Bible and lived by its principles while clinging to its promises. They went to church. They worshiped the Lord, and they prayed. I mean, they prayed! God knew their voices and used their voices; but more importantly, they knew God's voice. They walked in the fear of God and provoked the fear of God in me. These influencers of my life lived lives that were consistent, honorable, and true. In short, they were real in God—every day.

The influencers of my life stewarded their gift well. It's my hope that you and I will do the same with our gift. The words Jeremiah Johnson has written in this book will help us do that. They instruct us, providing us with insights in how to wield our gift in a way that pleases God and inspires others to do the same. As you hold this gift in your hand, you alone can choose how you will use it. Only you can determine to pay the price for being a godly influencer to this generation.

Karen Wheaton
Founder of The Ramp
Hamilton, Alabama

1

THE SECRET
TO INFLUENCE
AND LEGACY

I have come to the realization over the years that influence is not only a privilege and something that needs to be stewarded (handled, managed) well, but also brings with it a price to pay that is very costly and one that if I am honest, I was seriously naïve about early in my life. The pain and the glory of success, the gaining of friendships and the loss of them, dealing with the false accusation and constant criticism from the news and other sources, stewarding (overseeing, administering) the financial increase that influence brings, and trying to navigate it all with integrity and humility has become the greatest challenge of my life and ministry.

When I was in my mother's womb, she received a word from God about the prophetic call on my life to nations, that I would write books and be on television, and travel the world. Growing up with so many amazing prophetic words over my life produced many sincere goals and dreams of fulfilling them—but a complete lack of understanding of just how difficult it would be to accomplish them.

When you look at the Bible and church history, it is full of men and women who had been tested by obscurity and succeeded yet failed miserably the test of notoriety. In other words, many leaders have started off with success but did not finish well. Take King Uzziah for example, he served God and reigned in Israel for 52 years; but near the end of his life, he insisted on entering the temple and doing some things only permitted by priests. God inflicted the king with leprosy for the remainder of his time on the throne (see 2 Chronicles 26:16-23). How tragic!

Saul was hiding among the baggage in fear of recognition as a youth (1 Samuel 10:21-22), but as an older man and now crowned king, he was building public monuments to himself (1 Samuel 15:12). Young Saul started out so humble and pure, yet he finished prideful, arrogant, and disobedient to the Lord.

What about Samson? God set him apart as a Nazarite at birth, and his parents followed specific instructions to consecrate him in his youth (Judges 13). However, when he grew up and began to have influence in society, he fell prey to the seductions of Delilah. *Samson was consecrated in private but conquered in public.* Very few men and women have enjoyed the success of private devotion that translates to long-term public influence. Most of them were faithful in private for a period of years, but failed to walk in humility and integrity when public influence came.

In recent years, we have witnessed several leaders in the body of Christ all enjoy periods of tremendous success—yet there came a time in their ministries when they were publicly exposed for private sin. The devastation it has brought to so many lives, the disappointment it has unleashed on the Christian world, and the mockery it has brought to the name of Jesus has been absolutely heart wrenching. *The truth is that if we do not crucify our flesh privately, our flesh will crucify us publicly!*

I have personally learned over the years that around every corner of promotion and favor are surprise attacks by the enemy that we just are not prepared for. We learn through the life of Jesus that demonic spirits are always looking for the opportune time to attack us (Luke 4:13). Jealous people are consistently waiting to slander our character because our influence is growing and they want what we have. Friends and family who operate in witchcraft try to manipulate, control, and intimidate us into silence because they can't stand the success and favor we are walking in. People with a poverty mentality hate when financial blessing comes to us because we are obeying God.

While favor and promotion often draw surprise attacks from the devil, increasing influence also brings testing from the Lord to make sure our heart and motives remain pure.

The goal of God-given influence has never been to stroke our pride and ego, but rather to recognize the tremendous opportunity we have to lead a generation to Jesus. Discerning when God is trying to correct us through testing and when satan is trying to destroy us through demonic attack can become very difficult on our journey navigating influence.

To those who are hungry for public influence, are desperately self-promoting themselves online and in conversation, I would beseech them to think twice about what doors they are trying to knock down and what exactly they are asking for!

The facts are that influence is not what you think it is. It's dangerous, will steal your time, and try to take what's most precious to you—your family and real friends.

When hungry for public influence and promoting yourself online, you will become tempted to manage all your success at the expense of spending intimate time with God. If you fall into this trap, you will have an expanding public influence, but a shrinking heart that is losing its capacity to meet with God in the secret place. The constant phone calls, emails, and text messages will feed your ego and identity before you realize it. You will then have the potential of becoming entitled, demanding money and special treatment, and often, the only one who doesn't know you are full of yourself—is you.

The prophets, intercessors, and your real friends will weep over you and try to warn you. You might not listen to them because you have now put yourself above any need for correction and personal repentance!

Oh emerging generation of leaders with growing influence, I mourn for you because I know the journey ahead, and I know you won't make it without the fervent prayers of intercessors and spiritual leaders around you who will rebuke you and tell you the truth. You must be told the truth—that all the public influence means nothing if your marriage and family aren't healthy. And all the favor and promotion is in vain if you don't walk in humility and purity before God.

THE POWER OF INFLUENCE

There are many who struggle with the word *influence,* wrongly believing that it is not something that God wants them to have. As I briefly shared, public influence absolutely comes with its own set of challenges, difficulties, and a serious price; however, when properly stewarded (controlled/conducted) with the right heart and obedience to Jesus, influence can also become a powerful tool in the hands of the Lord to bring Him great glory. The Scriptures record many powerful stories in history when God gave men and women a tremendous sphere of influence for Kingdom purposes.

In the book of Esther, we find that God strategically raised up a Jewish woman as queen in order to spare her people. The power of influence was a gift given to Esther to save an entire generation and nation.

When Samuel the prophet walked into Bethlehem, the elders of the city came out trembling. They wanted to know if he came in peace or if he was there to deliver a hard word from God. The God-given prophetic influence Samuel had been gifted shook an entire city when he entered it. Wow!

What about Jesus Christ? There really is no argument that He was and is the most influential person in history. And the Bible that is written about His life and ministry is the best-selling book of all time!

Influence then is not a gift from God that we should reject, but rather embrace and thank Him for whatever and whomever He has called us to impact. The lives we can touch in our lifetime with influence is hard to fathom. Reverend Billy Graham saw approximately 3.2 million people saved by the gospel of Jesus Christ in his ministry. It is said that Reinhard Bonnke's ministry brought approximately 75 million souls to Christ. God is the One who gave them influence to reach millions—all for His glory!

FOLLOW JOHN'S EXAMPLE

The life and ministry of John the Baptist truly carries the fragrance of the power and price of influence. He was a man who preached out in the wilderness with great fervor and told people to repent; yet the Scriptures record, *"At that time Jerusalem was going out to him, and all Judea and all the region around the Jordan"* (Matthew 3:5 NASB). Notice the word *all.* Large crowds went out to the wilderness from Jerusalem, Judea, and around the Jordan River to hear John the Baptist preach an extremely hard message. Did John compromise his ministry because many people followed him, or had God given him public influence as a gift to reach the multitudes?

John's faithfulness to steward the influence God had given him and the ultimate price he paid with his life leaves us a powerful example of what it means to navigate the sphere of influence God has given each one of us. The following are five keys we can learn from that set John the Baptist apart in his generation:

1. John the Baptist had clarity concerning his message (Mark 1:3). John gave himself as a voice crying out in the wilderness. He was not content being an echo with another man's message. The clarity he possessed revealed the price that he was willing to pay to navigate the crowds that God had given him.

2. John the Baptist understood his assignment (John 1:27). Although John was growing in influence, he clearly recognized that he was just a forerunner for Jesus. When given an opportunity to go beyond his assignment, he refused and pointed the masses to Christ. Rather than promote himself, he pointed to Jesus and said, *"Behold, the Lamb of God, who takes away the sin of the world!"* (John 1:29 NASB).

3. John the Baptist possessed courage against opposition (Matthew 3:7). John often faced fierce opposition as he remained faithful to his calling. He was given a message of repentance and often confronted religious leaders regarding their hypocrisy and hidden sin. John possessed courage in the face of opposition because he feared God more than he feared humans.

4. John the Baptist was humble in heart (John 3:30). At a time in his ministry and influence where it would have been so easy to exalt himself and point to how many he had baptized or preached to, John humbled himself! In humility he declared to all who would listen to him, *"He* [Jesus] *must increase, but I must decrease"* (John 3:30 NASB). What a stunning example to anyone navigating the price and power of influence. Rather than chasing stardom, John ultimately would face martyrdom. Humility will grant you the heavenly rewards that pride will sabotage and take away!

5. John the Baptist lived a simple lifestyle (Mark 1:6). The way John dressed and even the food he ate protected him from the temptations that can come with growing influence. John was a simple man who did not live a lavish lifestyle or flaunt material possessions. It is so important that men and women with influence do not lose the fresh anointing upon their lives because they give vanity a place in their lives. As Lou Engle has said so well, "The times we live in demand that we fast and pray, yet all this generation wants to do is feast and play!"

Matthew 11:11 says that there was no one greater than John the Baptist born of a woman up until that time in history. What a stunning declaration! Greatness, therefore, is not found in the hearts of those who crave to be famous and influential. Rather, greatness is found in the hearts of those who crave servanthood and want Jesus to get all the glory. Just as God raised up a man of great influence in his generation named John the Baptist to prepare the earth for the first coming of Jesus Christ, so I believe God is raising up another generation of modern-day influencers in the spirit of John the Baptist who are going to prepare the earth for Christ's second coming.

REVIVAL HISTORY

In the days of John Wesley and George Whitefield (preachers of the First Great Awakening in the United States of America), the followers of George Whitefield came to him

SECRETS TO STEWARDING GOD'S VOICE IN A NEW ERA

and inquired as to how he would like to be remembered in history. (Wesley and his followers would eventually start the Methodist denomination.) How would George White-field desire to be remembered? Just like John the Baptist, the crowds were growing and all eyes were on him. I believe his profound answer reveals a secret to stewarding God's voice in this new era. Whitefield said:

> Let the name of Whitefield perish, but Christ be glorified. Let my name die everywhere, let even my friends forget me, if by that means the cause of the blessed Jesus may be promoted. But what is Calvin, or what is Luther? Let us look above names and parties; let Jesus be our all in all—So that He is preached. I care not who is upper-most. I know my place, even to be the servant of all. I am content to wait till the judgement day for the clearing up of my reputation; and after I am dead I desire no other epitaph than this, "Here lies G.W. What sort of man he was the great day will discover."[1]

The secret to the influence and legacy of men like John the Baptist and George Whitefield was their burning passion to see their names forgotten so that Jesus Christ could be made famous on earth. Are we ready to follow in their footsteps in this new era of history and steward the voice of God?

NOTE

1. Arnold Dallimore, *George Whitefield: God's Anointed Servant in the Great Revival of the Eighteenth Century* (Westchester, IL: Crossway, 1990), 154.

2

DON'T DESPISE YOUR YOUTH

I knew God called me to preach at 12 years old. I spoke to my father, who was pastoring, about this and he encouraged me to immediately witness to the poor and needy. I began faithfully going down to Lighthouse Mission in Indianapolis, Indiana, throughout my adolescent and teen years. It was a shelter for the homeless that had a midweek Bible study. The smells and sights of that place I will never forget. They graciously allowed me to minister there for years and serve the men dinner. I still have some of the cassette tapes of my messages on the love of God.

I graduated high school and went straight to Bible college. While there, I signed up for the "preaching teams" and quickly discovered I would be continually rotated between two venues: the juvenile prison for youth and a retired park for the elderly. For the next few years, I faithfully preached to old folks falling asleep on one weekend and on another weekend preached to demonized juveniles who screamed during the preaching and purposely flushed the toilets during prayer and altar calls. I also went on as many mission trips as I could where I would be exposed to extreme poverty and have the opportunity to preach the gospel to the poor.

There were no microphones, love offerings, social media fame, or livestreams. I never once thought I was being taken advantage of or overlooked. I sincerely believed I was being given the opportunity of a lifetime to share the sacred gospel with a lost and dying world.

Years and years of this faithful and mundane private preaching journey since I was 12 years old is what prepared me for the larger opportunities to minister that I have been given across the United States and around the world. Yes, I now preach to hundreds of thousands every year on large stages and across social media, but most don't know my story.

As I look out at the landscape of the Christian world online and at the conferences where I speak, I truly grieve beyond words at the mindsets and conversations I often have with people who dream of gaining more influence. So many people reach out to me every week, hoping that I will ask them to speak at one of our conferences or connect them with one of my famous friends.

When I suggest they begin preaching to the poor, ministering to the elderly, or sharing in the prisons as I did for years, they think I am trying to insult them. They get offended and accuse me of not seeing their gifting or value. They want the camera, they want the travel itinerary, and how could anyone even suggest ministering where they can't pay you?

EARLY MINISTRY LESSONS

I was hired with a full-time salary at 20 years old to work as the young adult and associate pastor of a large Assemblies of God church while I completed my Bible degree in college. I was thrown into an extremely demanding schedule for almost two years straight where I preached many Wednesday nights, every Friday night to the young adults, and one Sunday morning a month at the church. I constantly counseled, discipled, evangelized, and visited the sick. I was the first one there to open the building and the last one to leave most days. I was totally committed, loved the body of believers, and knew there was so much more God had for us.

One day I suddenly had an encounter with God where I realized this intense period of time was the training ground for something weightier, something that would require even more of me. I began to feel the tension, the frustration, and even the agony at times of constantly serving another man's vision. My heart started turning sour toward

The desire for *FAME*,

the sense of *ENTITLEMENT*,

and the *LOVE OF MONEY*

IS A CANCER

attempting to kill so many to

whom God has given influence

in this generation.

the senior pastor. I thought I was some big shot ready for more responsibility and influence.

Then a lightning bolt came! A word from the throne room of Heaven that caused my knees to instantly hit the ground. "Jeremiah!" God said, "You must be careful how you treat and serve the man I have set over you, because how you treat him as a leader now will be how people treat you one day as you lead."

I immediately purposed in my heart to serve even harder, to sacrifice even more, to go above and beyond what was required. The truth is that many of us have to serve a Saul to get the Saul out of us! Isn't God so kind?

CHURCH PLANTING

I planted my first church at 22 years old after completing almost two years of service at the Assemblies of God church. My wife and I graduated Bible college, got married, and started the church out of our living room all within a nine-month period. We were heavily persecuted because of our youth, inexperience, and passion for God. However, He was truly with us in those early years of pioneering.

Three years into church planting and at 25 years old, I was doing my best to steward the small influence God had given me in the local church. One day, I was sitting at my

The truth is

that many of us

HAVE TO SERVE A SAUL

to get the Saul

OUT OF US!

desk soaked in sweat because we could not afford to air condition the offices during the week. Reading my Bible, I remember looking over at the thermostat and it was 83 degrees. Suddenly the glory of God filled my office. I got on my knees quickly and the voice of God immediately spoke to me saying, "I'm sending you, Jeremiah." I honestly had absolutely no clue what He meant.

Almost overnight, doors, opportunities, connections, and invitations that I never asked for or could dream of began to open up all across the United States and around the world. Since that encounter at 25, I have now preached in 43 states and 25 nations. Our ministry receives close to 400 invitations every year requesting that I come minister, and we have never advertised any of it.

All by God's grace, I have preached in stadiums and large outdoor events, been on television many times and even featured in the movies, written best-selling books, and touched millions of people online with the gospel of Jesus Christ. There have been so many seasons when I have asked myself, "How did I even get here?"

God's honest truth is that I was totally unprepared for all the national stages and popularity, the offers that came with the success, the hidden trials and testing behind the scenes, the fierce persecution and loads of hate mail, and all that comes with increasing influence. Being constantly pulled in every direction, trying to discern the voice of God, feeling the unbelievable pressure of the applause and people's promised finances, juggling a growing local church and traveling ministry, maintaining a healthy marriage and home life have all been weighty and impossible challenges to overcome without the grace of God and serious prayer and accountability.

It's still so strange meeting thousands of saints from all around the world who have huge aspirations and ambitions of having national and global influence. My personal experiences of the power and price of influence has caused me to sit many of them down and challenge them to examine the motives and intentions of their hearts. Is their marriage and family prepared for what happens when greater influence comes?

I truly believe that God loves to give influence to His sons and daughters. However, if there is a crack in the foundation of our character and private life in Jesus, what God intends to bless us with will actually crush us. The very spotlight that we crave is the very spotlight that will expose our hidden sin if we are not right with God.

When Jesus Christ walked the earth, He Himself was perfected through trials, temptations, and testings. His ultimate destiny was sacrifice, redemption, and offering forgiveness to those who crucified Him. Should those with influence not have the same ambitions? When God gives influence to individuals, it is intended to increase their capacity to bring great glory and honor to Jesus. He alone is worthy of all adoration and applause!

PURCHASING A
CHURCH HOME

After six grueling years of church planting out of our living room with no denominational backing or funding and
beginning with only a handful of people, we purchased a
multimillion-dollar facility as our forever church home in
Lakeland, Florida. All to the praise and glory of God! Being
28 years old at the time, I could have never dreamed that
God would perform such a mighty miracle in our midst.

It truly was a series of supernatural events where God
established us in our city as a sign and a wonder. He chose
a young man like me who made so many mistakes along
the way to blaze a path for a young generation of pioneers
even in their 20s and 30s. Yes, there is a dear price to pay
for influence. However, God is always faithful and He will
do what He said He will do.

The words of Paul to Timothy have always been special
to me as he wrote to his young mentee son, *"Let no one look
down on your youthfulness, but rather in speech, conduct,
love, faith, and purity, show yourself an example of those
who believe"* (1 Timothy 4:12 NASB).

A BIG SPANKING
FROM GOD

When I first began to travel and minister, God immediately opened some larger-than-expected doors for me to walk through. I quickly found myself preaching on large platforms and in mega-churches that I honestly had no idea how I got there. Over time, I believe I was developing a sense of entitlement and even arrogance that had to be addressed and corrected. In God's great mercy, He decided to step in and give me a big spanking on the road.

One day I received an invitation to preach at a large multicampus church in Tennessee. As I ministered, the power of God was so strong during the night meetings that I could hardly stand. I preached at several of the campuses and then the big Sunday morning service came.

I received a surprise phone call in the hotel early that morning from the pastor. He said he believed God spoke to him that I was to go to his friend's church that morning and then return Sunday night for the final service of the weekend.

I was picked up several hours later and headed to this unknown church. It was not on the schedule and all a surprise. I remember the scene like it was yesterday. It was a church plant in the middle of nowhere Tennessee with less than 20 people in an old middle school gymnasium.

As I sat in the chair on the front row during praise and worship, I was fuming. Didn't they know who I was? I preached in mega-churches and people drove to hear me from hundreds of miles away. I was so "anointed."

All of a sudden, I felt the tangible grief of God on my neck and His stern voice whisper in my ear, "Oh, so you think you're a big shot now, Jeremiah? I allowed you to taste a high level of success early on and now your entitlement and pride is a stench in My nostrils. If you are too big to preach to the small, then you are too small to preach to the big. If you do not repent of your sin, I will strip My anointing from your life and humiliate you before the people. I want you to now get up and preach as if there are five thousand people here, and don't you dare take the love offering when they try and give you one."

The holy fear of God hit me in that moment and I fell out of the chair onto the hardwood floor and wept bitterly before Him. It was a spanking that I desperately needed and a clear course correction that by the grace of God I believe I am still on. Since that day, I vowed to God that I would purposely schedule ministry trips every year to small churches and preach and prophesy my guts out and not ask for a thing. God told me to never require a certain honorarium to minister as long as I lived. Period.

To this day, people show up to some of the very small churches and church plants where I purposely choose to minister and say, "Jeremiah, why in the world are you here?

I just saw you preach to five thousand people last weekend?" I tell them all the same thing. "I preach to whoever and wherever God leads me. I humble myself in obedience to Him, stewarding the prophetic anointing that He has given me."

We all need spankings from God. It's His great mercy and love. King David put it like this, *"Before I was afflicted, I went astray..."* (Psalm 119:67 NASB). To those with growing influence, if you are tasting great levels of success and open doors, be very careful that you are not confusing the anointing with your ego. *Open doors are not necessarily a sign of God's favor, they can actually simply be the instruments He uses to test the motivations and intentions of your heart.* God is ALWAYS watching!

THE SEDUCTION OF INFLUENCE

Navigating growing influence as a young man has been indescribable at times. Staring into video cameras that literally broadcast what you prophesy around the world, standing on national stages under the spotlight and having all eyes on you, preaching from the platforms of large churches looking out into a sea full of people desperate for a word from God, and being featured in various national newspapers and magazines has brought me more fear of the Lord than excitement.

The pressures, applause, temptations, offers, seductions, compromise, identity crisis, and insecurity are untold. Most saints honestly can't even imagine or relate.

What I have discovered in talking with many Christians over the years is that we all think we would speak the truth without compromise—until we actually stand on those huge stages and national platforms, until we are offered major money and open doors, until we actually experience the torrent and barrage of deception and pressure to finally realize the cost of speaking the truth without compromise.

Personally, these have been some of the hardest choices I have ever had to make and these are not one-time choices either. To refuse to be bought with fame, money, and applause when it is constantly being shoved in your face is incredibly difficult.

As someone navigating this extremely dangerous path of influence, can I beseech you to intercede for those you see being promoted and given increasing favor? I know it appears that they have it all going on, but the truth is that the devil is looking for a foothold that he can turn into a stronghold. Without our fervent cries for protection and purity for people of influence, the tendency for them to become prideful, arrogant, compromised, and polluted is very high.

If more people only understood what I'm even talking about, they would stop constantly craving platforms and microphones. It's one thing to not care about a platform because you have never been given one, and it's another to walk in great influence yet refuse to be pimped and prostituted.

TROUBLING OBSERVATIONS

One of the most troubling observations I have made over the years of being around many successful leaders in the body of Christ is the fact that those who follow them closely are typically unaware of the price their leaders have paid and are paying to walk in what they carry.

I know way too many staff members, personal assistants, and close followers of key leaders in the body of Christ who simply enjoy the benefits of their leaders overcoming severe trial and crushing, just so fresh oil could be poured out through their own lives and ministry.

This deception runs deep because it causes these staff members, assistants, and congregants to live vicariously through the success of their leaders and then half of them think they can do it better—all the while they are riding the coattails of the leaders who are being crushed so they can get paid and enjoy the overflow. It's awful!

If you have the honor and privilege of serving along-side a successful leader in the body of Christ, I want to challenge you not to allow the price they paid and are pay-ing to deceive you into thinking you are right with God and paying a price yourself. You must refuse to live vicariously through their sacrifices and start making your own. Their notoriety does not make you notable. Their history in God does not replace the need for you to make your own. You are not entitled to the open doors He has given them. Stop looking for the fast pass at Disney World and learn how to pay your own dues.

This circumstance often manifests when those who have served successful leaders or sat under their ministries step out on their own and suddenly realize they are not ready, nor do they walk in the kind of favor and anointing they thought they would. This is a direct result of assumption, deception, and entitlement. These folks spent years follow-ing a leader who was paying a dear price without realizing they were called to pay one too. Although they can mimic the lingo they heard from their leader, there is no oil on their life because they have never fully surrendered to the call.

Rather than ask seasoned leaders about all their vic-tories and success, please ask them about all the hell and warfare they endure so that you and thousands of others can enjoy "their ministry." Sincerely ask them if they really think you are paying a price to get your own oil, or are you just constantly shoplifting theirs?

Days are quickly coming to the Kingdom of God when just one leader will not lay down his or her life for the church or movement but entire groups of people are going to be crushed together so that new wine can be poured forth in the body of Christ.

SEASONED LEADERS AND PRIVATE TABLES

I have had the privilege of being invited to many private tables and meetings with well-known and seasoned leaders in the body of Christ. Looking around the room as a young man to men and women who have been faithful and very successful for decades in various spheres of influence, one question deep inside my heart has always gripped me, "Why am I here?"

Rather than being left to myself with this pressing and oftentimes troubling question, the seasoned and successful leaders have actually answered it themselves before I can even ask. And they have always been unanimous in their responses. It has stunned me again and again.

"Jeremiah, you have been invited as a young man to these private tables and gatherings because of only two things: 1. You have a proven track record of building something righteous, and 2. You possess character and integrity that has been tested."

Meditating on these two exactly-the-same responses that I have been given by more than 25 senior leaders over the years has caused me to want to reach out today and encourage so many young leaders in this generation who desire to have access to and be mentored by seasoned and influential leaders.

My two pieces of advice from my personal experiences are:

> **1.** Rather than just posting great "revelation" online and videos talking about how much you are traveling and doing for the Kingdom of God, give yourself to actually building something for the Kingdom. In other words, where are the addresses of the churches you say you have planted and what are the names of the leaders you claim to have discipled and sent out? Where are the recommendations from the leaders of the churches and conferences where you have spoken? You are claiming to be a pioneer, but what exactly have you pioneered? You say you are a "voice," but is anyone actually listening to you?
>
> Calling yourself a "prophet to the nations" when no one in this nation has ever heard of you is not impressive. Claiming you are a "master apostle" with 50 people attending your church over the past 20 years is not something to boast about.
>
> Declaring that you have won "millions" to Christ on YouTube isn't going to give you

SECRETS TO STEWARDING GOD'S VOICE IN A NEW ERA

credibility among senior leaders. Seasoned leaders are looking for verifiable evidence that you have a track record of faithfulness and blossoming fruit in your life and ministry. They want to know to whom you are accountable. They want to know in what church you are planted and serving. They are not impressed with what you think is wrong with the Church. They want to see what you have built as the solution to the problem. Posting conference flyers is nice, but are the altars full and lives being transformed? Are you really making disciples?

2. I never in my life have been told at these private table gatherings with seasoned and influential leaders that the reason why I have been invited was because I have a large social media following, can prophesy, and work miracles. They have all said the same thing, "We have investigated your marriage and family and found you to be a faithful husband and father. We have seen you own your mistakes and repent."

Character and integrity are highly valued among seasoned leaders. You do not have to be perfect, but walking in humility is key. Seasoned leaders value the *fruit* of the Holy Spirit far above the *gifts* of the Holy Spirit. When they detect pride and arrogance, they know you have not gone through enough testing and crushing to be trusted.

I hope my personal experiences and interactions that I have just shared will encourage and challenge many young leaders. Let's do less talking and more building. Before we go win the world, let's make sure we are winning at home. Instead of talking about all the problems in the Church and nations, let's actually give ourselves to developing solutions and discipling men and women. The truth is that many young leaders need to spend way less time online and way more time getting real Kingdom work done behind the scenes. God is looking for a generation of young influencers who have more than the *language* of change but actually possess the *lifestyle* of it.

PRAYER AND ACTIVATION

Whether you are young in age or older in years and are new to accepting the call God has on your life to influence the world around you, I want to pray for you and activate supernatural faith and boldness in your life. If God could use a young 20-something like me to successfully plant churches, travel and minister around the world, and speak on television and write books, He can absolutely use your life for His glory! In the following chapters, I share some powerful stories and keys to help you accomplish all that God has called you to be and do.

Let's pray:

God, I thank You for who You have created me to be. I accept the call that You have given me to influence the world around me. Please help me not to despise my youth and not to partner with unbelief. God, I ask that You would release supernatural favor and finance to accomplish Your will. Keep me humble and pure, as I always keep You at the center of my life, marriage, and family. In Jesus's name I pray. Amen!

3

THE DANGERS OF CELEBRITY CHRISTIANITY

W e are living in a very sobering and glorious era in the global Church when God is
measuring where churches, ministries, and
individuals stand regarding biblical issues—specifically
concerning abortion, sexual immorality, drunkenness, and
false doctrine.

One of the greatest blessings of these current times is
that we are going to witness healthy and necessary division in the global Church like never before. Please listen
carefully. While satan seeks to cause division in the Church
using tactics such as false accusation, slander, deception,
and more, this is *not* the healthy and necessary division
that God has shown me is coming.

What the Holy Spirit is revealing to me is found in 1 Corinthians 11:19 (AMP) where Paul writes, *"for [doubtless]*

there have to be factions among you, so that those who are of approved character may be clearly recognized among you." Another translation says it this way, *"But, of course, there must be divisions among you so that you who have God's approval will be recognized"* (1 Corinthians 11:19 NLT).

There is going to be tremendous unity taking place in these days, however, the factions and divisions that Paul speaks of actually have to happen *before* real unity can take place. In other words: the sheep must be separated from the goats, those who love truth must be separated from those who love deception, those who support abortion and same-sex marriage must be separated from those who choose life and define marriage between one man and one woman, *before* real unity can take place.

What does all of this mean?

It means we must prepare ourselves right now for the greatest shaking, exposure, and division in the global Church that we have ever seen in our lifetime. Again, I am not speaking concerning satan's attacks in the body that are based on lies, false accusation, and deception. What I am prophesying about is exposure and healthy division coming from God as a gift to His global Church so we can recognize the difference between the holy and the profane, the difference between those who love God and those who love the world.

When churches, ministries, and individuals get exposed for hidden sin and wickedness, there is naturally an extraordinary sense of grief, betrayal, hurt, and devastation among those who followed their leadership. While this response is expected, the Holy Spirit is trying to encourage, strengthen, and comfort us. He is enlightening us that when we see these things take place, we can respond appropriately. The Holy Spirit desires to bring the global Church into extraordinary unity, but we must accept that one of the ways He does this is by releasing cleansing judgment so we can recognize the difference between the precious and the vile (1 Peter 4:17). A holy separation is coming to the house of God, and it is going to be such a gift to those willing to discern and receive it.

God says, "Prepare your hearts My people! Do not be discouraged, alarmed, or even shocked by the shaking and exposure that is coming; rather, give thanks for the clarity and discernment that will come. You must get ready to decide what and who you love more. Do you love men and their ministries more than you love Me?"

NAVIGATING CELEBRITY CHRISTIANITY

As mentioned previously, I have been invited on numerous occasions to sit down in private with many influential leaders over the past two decades. Several of these leaders have come with great caution every time, saying, "Jeremiah, we see the gift and passion, but you cannot keep speaking out on certain issues if you want your platform and the crowds to get even bigger." Honestly, this "caution" always perplexed me, and I walked away with deep grief and tears on many occasions.

You see, I was being constantly counseled and advised that when I reached a certain realm of influence and leadership, I would have to be very guarded concerning certain issues. I was told to specifically stop preaching on:

1. Deliverance

2. Repentance

3. Holiness

4. Abortion

5. Sexual Immorality

I was told that those five subjects would cause the most controversy and offense as I reached the "top." With great fasting, prayer, and incredible inner turmoil, I chose to reject the advice of multiple famous Christian leaders and refused to compromise my messages to the best of my abilities. When God asked me to preach to the masses on how the shedding of innocent blood and sexual immorality bring His judgment to nations, I did. When I was being interviewed on live television and could have watered down key biblical issues, I instead called for repentance, deliverance, and holiness.

When I was offered large sums of money to stay silent, I spoke out and paid a dear price. Since when was Jesus more concerned about protecting His influence and platform than He was speaking the truth and pleasing His Father?

I share my personal journey now with tears to say this:

> To those who have a realm of influence now or who believe they will one day, *never* allow the size of your platform to change your message! You must refuse to be bought! When you make those painful choices and pass the tests—there will be many—you will become a great threat and thorn in the flesh to those with even more influence who have compromised their messages. You will be avoided by many and slandered in green rooms. The "wisdom" some will give you concerning your future will actually seek to smother the fire God put inside your bones. Your commitment to a standard of righteousness will be wrongly labeled "legalism."
>
> Whether it's speaking to ten people or a million, whether there's no love offering or you get $50,000 honorariums, I encourage you, *do not compromise* what God has placed in your heart. And please be aware that just as older and

more influential leaders have hunted me down and told me to be more positive over and over again and just preach more encouraging messages, they will come for you too and ask you to wear their armor. When they do, know that I am praying for you! Be bold, be courageous, and may the only thing that changes in your life as you gain more influence and a greater platform is a deeper measure of conviction, prayer, fasting, and intimacy with Jesus Christ!

A PROPHETIC WARNING DREAM

God gave my friend, who is a pastor, a powerful prophetic dream one night that is a warning to anyone seeking to gain more influence with the wrong heart and motives. Derrick Hawkins writes and says:

I had a dream one night that has challenged and served as a bit of caution. This dream reflected what I would call the spirit that seeks to attack our churches and clergy. It's a spirit of celebrity Christianity.

There were three levels in my dream. The first level is where everyone in the dream initially gathered. We were all in a lobby setting. Everyone present was extremely cordial and very welcoming. It was genuine starting off. Everyone was gathered together to enjoy a meal. While we were waiting for the meal to be prepared, everyone was hanging out, talking, and catching up.

In the room, there were three types of people. There were those who had massive influence, those who were becoming influential, and those who had influence but chose to walk the *narrow* path. The last group of people were sitting on the sidelines observing those who had had influence and those who desired to become influential.

The second level of the dream is when things began to change. People who were *initially* genuine shepherds started to become filled with lust, pride, and deceit. As the wait for the food continued, people began to gravitate toward people who were the most influential in the room. It was very subtle at first. It wasn't harmful initially. The leaders all still had very genuine motives. However, the longer the meal took to come, the more people gathered around the influencers in the room.

The third level is where the dream really became disturbing. By the time the food was prepared, we all begin to travel up an escalator. During that time, a separation began to take place. By this time, people gathered around their *preference.* They gathered around the leader who they *aspired to be like.* What started as a genuine gathering became divisive and extremely personality driven. The meal was never eaten, the servers who served were disregarded and disrespected, and the tables that were prepared were abandoned.

The influencers who had influence but chose the narrow path were *isolated* from those who had massive influence. Very *few* people gathered around them. The crowd followed the influencers and abandoned those on the narrow path. All of sudden the scene shifted from this extravagant building where everyone gathered to an airport.

All of the influencers rejected the meal that was prepared and ran to their next engagement. As people began to follow the influential leaders, they all went to board a plane. The plane crashed. The influencers who *desired* influence were being followed into the room and boarded the plane that crashed. The only ones who *remained* were the remnant influencers who chose the narrow path.

For the ones who are seeking notoriety over intimacy, the Lord is calling us back to the table. For the ones who feel overlooked because you don't fit, you are right where you need to be. For the ones who have used their influence for manipulation, deceit, and greed, the Lord wants you to come back to Him. For the ones who are in the crowd chasing what we feel will take us to our next level without intimacy with the Holy Spirit, I pray the eyes of hearts and minds would be enlightened.

Celebrity Christianity is idol worship.

Do *not* let it become your ***golden calf.***

This revival will not be on the shoulders of man but through the *counsel* of God. Lord, forgive us if we have abandoned Your table of communion for platform and opportunities. Matthew 7:13-14 (NIV) says, *"Enter through the narrow gate. For wide is the gate and broad is the road that leads to destruction, and many enter through it. But small is the gate and narrow the road that leads to life, and only a few find it."*

MINISTRY ADDICTION

Pursuing ministry opportunity and following Jesus Christ are *not* the same thing.

An addiction to applause, platforms, microphones, and ministry connections and networking is as addicting as crack cocaine. The pursuit of "ministry" is the premier cover-up of a dysfunctional marriage, family, and personal life. The pursuit of "ministry" allows many to hide their sin because they measure their success in God based on the open doors they have been given, not on their character and integrity or even if their own family loves and appreciates them.

The truth is that God is way more interested in changing us on the inside (character) than using us on the outside (ministry).

Our agreement with this statement can only be found in whether we value the prayer room more than a platform. If we are daydreaming of speaking before the masses instead of standing on the sea of glass and gazing at the beauty of Jesus, our priorities are skewed, and we are more than likely consumed with an addiction to ministry.

(How I wish I was taught about character, prayer, fasting, having a devotional life, and developing a healthy family life while I earned a four-year Bible degree! Instead I was instructed on how to network, market, build a ministry platform, and create a culturally relevant church. It took years to get delivered from these worldly mindsets and practices.)

I see a generation of influencers actually having character that matches the anointing upon their lives. This fruit can only be forged in the fires of prayer and devotion. I don't believe God is interested in who we know and what doors we walk through. He wants to know if we are praying, fasting, blessing our enemies, giving to the poor, and loving our spouses and children. (The stuff that doesn't sell books and make good YouTube videos.) For all the major addictions being addressed in the Church today, why is being addicted to ministry never discussed or even exposed?

CHURCH LEADERS—WE ARE NOT SUPERSTARS

The president of Southeastern Baptist Theological Seminary, Daniel Akin, addressed the dangers of celebrity Christianity in his following article title, "Brothers, We Are Not Superstars":[1]

> Jesus summarizes the purpose of his incarnation in Mark 10:45 when he says, "Even the Son of Man came not to be served, but to serve, and to give his life as a ransom for many." This profound and crucial statement, which weds the "Son of Man" title of Daniel 7:13–14 to the "suffering Servant" of Isaiah 52–53, and redefines what kind of Messiah-Savior our Lord would be, comes on the heels of James's and John's request that Jesus would give them seats on his right and left in Glory (verse 37). James and John are crystal clear in their intentions and goal: they

want status, not service. They want the position of a king, not the calling of a slave. They want to be looked up to, honored, and revered. They wanted to be superstars, not servants.

Tragically, today, when it comes to the ministry, the standards and criteria for success are too often culled from the world, and not from the Word of God. To deny this is to play the ostrich, stick our head in the sand, and simply ignore the massive evidence that swirls around us. Allow me to share what I see.

Evangelicals have their cult-heroes and cult followings. This is true both inside and outside the local church. We have our groupies who pine after their "Christian rock stars." Such stars are given almost infallible status, at least by their devoted fans, and if they are not careful, they may begin to believe what blogs, fans, and fellow superstars say.

Suddenly, the green monster of pride sneaks into their lives and an attitude of entitlement begins to transform a once gracious and humble servant into a hulk-like prima donna who less and less resembles the simple carpenter from Galilee. Subtly, over time, I convince myself that I deserve a six-figure salary. I deserve to live in a big home and drive an expensive car. I deserve to have people wait on me hand and foot and respond immediately to my every request.

Furthermore, they can expect to receive a quick and painful tongue-lashing if they move too slowly or fail to meet my exalted expectations. Why, I may even fire them for not measuring up to my personal expectations.

I become too important and my time is too valuable to meet with common people, people who cannot help me further my agenda. I am too busy in "my ministry" to respond to letters, answer emails, return phone calls or schedule appointments. And amazingly, I become almost self-righteous in defending my lifestyle, all my perks, and my prideful behavior because what I do is valuable to the kingdom and I've earned the right to be treated as one of its kings.

I wish what I have written to this point was theoretical or at least hyperbolic. Sadly, it isn't. As someone who has been in the Christian ministry for 35 years, and who battles daily the green monster of pride, I have seen and continue to see this superstar mentality and lifestyle far too often among a number of current day pastors. You see, I am now a seminary president who, if not careful, can get caught up in all of this "malarkey." I am easily seduced by the sirens who feed a superstar mentality that knows nothing of the way of Jesus.

So, what biblical counsel and wisdom can help keep our heads out of the clouds and our feet on the ground where "real people" live? Let me offer one avenue of Scriptural exhortation that may help.

Keep continually before you the biblical model of leadership. We are not CEOs. We are not professionals. Brothers, we are shepherds—and under-shepherds at that. We are servant-leaders. First Peter 5:2 instructs us to "shepherd the flock of God that is among you." The word "shepherd" is an imperative receiving the force of a command. Shepherds who follow in the footsteps of the "Good Shepherd" (John 10:11), the "Chief Shepherd" (1 Peter 5:4), the "Great Shepherd" (Heb. 13:20), will love and lead their sheep. They will not drive them and use them and make ungodly carnal demands of them. They will continually remind themselves that they tend over "the flock of God" and not their own.

They also understand it is the "flock of God among you." That means they live with their sheep, they spend time with their sheep, they know their sheep, they care for their sheep. I once heard a famous and well-known pastor brag about the fact he had never had a single meal in the home of one of his members nor had he ever invited any of his members into his home for one. When I asked him why, he simply responded, "I never wanted to get that close to any of my people." Words cannot express how this broke my heart. It still grieves me to this day.

Brothers, we never have been and never will be superstars. We are lowly shepherds, servants of the "Great Shepherd of the sheep." One day we will give him an account for the souls we are keeping watch over (Heb. 13:17). May we by his grace and for his glory do so with joy and a clear conscience, serving him and his sheep "honorably in all things" (Heb. 13:18).

BECOMING POOR IN SPIRIT

How can leaders with growing influence avoid the pitfalls and trappings of celebrity Christianity? One of the main answers is found in embracing the poor-in-spirit reality that Jesus Christ taught in Matthew 5:3 (NIV). He said, *"Blessed are the poor in spirit, for theirs is the kingdom of heaven."* If there ever was a Man with incredible influence who walked in humility and obedience to the Father—it was Jesus Christ.

Oswald Chambers calls the first beatitude in Matthew 5, "the first principle of the Kingdom." He goes on to warn, "As long as we have a conceited, self-righteous notion that we can do the thing if God will help us, God has to allow us to go on until we break the neck of our ignorance over some obstacle, then we are willing to come and receive from Him."[2]

What exactly does it mean to be poor in spirit? Becoming poor in spirit is embracing and confessing our great need of God. It's giving Him all the credit, honor, and glory for anything and everything that we have ever accomplished.

Years ago, I was in a time of prayer and meditation with my friend Corey Russell. We were praying into Revelation chapter 4. This chapter of the Bible explains how there are 24 elders and four living creatures in the throne room of God who worship Jesus night and day. As we prayed, I felt prompted to ask the Holy Spirit a question. I said, "What are the rules in the throne room?" He said, "Jeremiah, there is only one rule in the throne room and it is this: There are no crowns allowed."

This revelation hit my heart with such impact that I began to weep and shout! There really is only One who is worthy and His name is Jesus Christ. When we see Him for who He really is, our crowns, which can represent all our human accomplishments and accolades, pale in comparison with the beauty of this Man, Jesus.

When people with influence boast in their own strength about all they have done, it truly is a sign that they have not been in close proximity to Jesus. Paul the apostle received this same revelation. As a man with great influence and accomplishments, he boldly declared, *"I count all things to be loss in view of the surpassing value of knowing Christ Jesus my Lord, for whom I have suffered the loss of all things, and count them mere rubbish, so that I may gain Christ"* (Philippians 3:8 NASB).

Martin Lloyd-Jones says that "poor in spirit" is "ultimately a man's attitude toward himself.... This is something which is not only not admired by the world; it is despised by it. You will never find a greater antithesis to the worldly spirit and outlook than that which you find in this verse. What emphasis the world places on its belief in self-reliance, self-confidence, and self-expression!"

Lloyd-Jones continues: "The Sermon on the Mount, in other words, comes to us and says, 'There is the mountain that you have to scale, the heights you have to climb, and the first thing you must realize, as you look at that mountain which you are told you must ascend, is that you cannot do it, that you are utterly incapable in and of yourself, and that any attempt to do it in your own strength is proof positive that you have not understood it."[3]

A HUMBLE MAN WITH INFLUENCE

An incredible example of a man who truly confessed and lived a lifestyle of spiritual bankruptcy before God was

William Carey, known as the "Father of Modern Missions."
Listen to this story of his life and allow the Holy Spirit to
minister to your heart:

> When the fire of 1812 destroyed dozens of his
> precious manuscripts, William Carey didn't
> blame the devil. He said, "How unsearchable
> are the ways of God!"
>
> And then he accused himself of too much
> self-congratulation in his labors and said, "The
> Lord has smitten us, He had a right do to so,
> and we deserve His corrections."
>
> When he had outlived four of his comrades
> in mission, he wrote back to Andrew Fuller, "I
> know not why so fruitless a tree is preserved;
> but the Lord is too wise to err."
>
> When he died in 1834 in Serampore, India,
> a simple tablet was put on his grave with the
> words he requested. And when you hear these
> I want you to ask: What was William Carey's
> secret? How could he persevere for forty years
> over all obstacles—as a homely man, suffering
> from recurrent fever, limping for years from
> an injury in 1817, and yet putting the entire
> Bible into six languages and parts of it into
> 29 other languages—what was the secret of
> this man's usefulness and productivity for the
> kingdom?
>
> The tablet on his grave reads:

WILLIAM CAREY

Born August 17the, 1761

Died June 9the, 1834

A wretched, poor, and helpless worm,

On Thy kind arms I fall.

His secret was in the last line of his epitaph: "On Thy kind arms I fall." This was his secret in dying and this was his secret in living. He cast himself—poor, helpless, despicable—on the kind arms of God, for he knew the promise of Jesus: "Blessed are the poor in spirit, for to them belong the merciful and mighty arms of the King of Kings."[4]

God is truly raising up a generation of men and women with great influence. These individuals recognize that there is only one celebrity—His name is Jesus Christ. It is their supreme joy, honor, and delight to confess their great need of Him. They spend long hours in prayer and worship, staring at the One who sits on the throne. These influencers choose to put their constant boast and trust in the Lord. They understand that the bigger doors that God opens up for them, the greater their responsibility is to share the truth at all costs. Influencers with the touch of Heaven on their lives will never sacrifice the truth of the gospel for the sake of more fans and followers. They are just too in

SECRETS TO STEWARDING GOD'S VOICE IN A NEW ERA

love with Jesus to exchange temporary applause for eternal glory!

Having a greater desire to please God than obtain human praise will protect and preserve people with influence all the days of their lives. *Jesus never sacrificed truth for popularity.*

NOTES

1. Daniel L. Akin, "Brothers, We Are Not Superstars," *DesiringGod,* October 30, 2012; https://www.desiringgod .org/articles/brothers-we-are-not-superstars; accessed July 3, 2024.

2. Oswald Chambers, *Studies in the Sermon on the Mount* (Gideon House Books, 2016).

3. D. Martyn Lloyd-Jones, *Studies in the Sermon on the Mount* (Grand Rapids, MI: Eerdmans Publishing Co, 1971).

4. John Piper, "Blessed are the Poor in Spirit Who Mourn," *Desiring God*, 2 February 1986.

4

HEALTHY COMMUNITY AND ACCOUNTABILITY

Influence brings with it not only the ability to have great success but also the capacity to fail miserably. It's possible to influence many in a positive way or have a negative effect on the masses. Whether someone has long-term success or not is primarily measured by the healthy community and accountability they have placed around their lives. The need to have the right people around you as a person of influence can never be overstated. The great difficulty as you grow in influence is determining who actually loves you for the person you are and who just wants to be in close proximity to you because they secretly or openly have an agenda to destroy you.

Speaking very vulnerably, I have no idea where I, my marriage, and family would be without a healthy local church over the years and several key spiritual mothers and fathers who have helped us navigate not only grow-ing influence but also the spiritual warfare that has come along with it. We have been tremendously blessed to have people invested in our lives where there are shared dreams, struggles, and victories. We also have had to set up boundaries in many seasons as we realized that some we had hoped would become friends were actually deter-mined to destroy us.

THE LOCAL CHURCH

I treasure the local church. It has been the primary place God has used to humble me, heal me, keep me human, and taught me valuable lessons that I walk with to this day. Having influence on a national and global level is a bless-ing. When you travel and speak at various churches and events, there is a level of respect and honor that comes with it that requires little to no effort on your part. For many, you are larger than life from their perspective. This can be a good thing or actually lead to great deception.

While being honored and respected in many arenas, this naturally comes with people who don't know who you really are. People can love my preaching and prophesying because it impacts their lives at various venues, but only the people in my local church who I do life with really know who I am. The local elders and friends get a front-row seat to my marriage and how I parent my kids. They alone have the ability to actually really see whether my influence is producing fruit or not.

In other words, when I travel and minister, I "impact" people temporarily; but only where I am planted and labor on a weekly basis reveals the real "fruit" of who I am and what God has called me to be and do. Distinguishing the difference between impact and fruit is very important.

The great danger of traveling and online ministry in the body of Christ today is that so many with Christian influence online and at speaking engagements rarely have anyone on a local level who actually knows them for real. We can all fake it on social media and stages, but where are the local church leaders and friends who can actually vouch for our character, marriage, and family?

There is a lack of discernment today in the body of Christ that is scary. The metrics we use to determine success are worldly and carnal. Making money and becoming famous is not the goal of following Jesus—obedience to His voice and calling on our life is the goal. If financial blessing and reaching the multitudes becomes part of our inheritance, then we should thank God for it. However, it should never lead us to isolation away from the local church and elders, cause us to grow in pride and arrogance, or worse cause us to sacrifice our marriage and kids on the altar of growing our platform.

Making *MONEY* and

becoming *FAMOUS*

IS NOT THE GOAL

of following Jesus.

HEALTHY COMMUNITY AND ACCOUNTABILITY

We have witnessed one leader after another in the body of Christ fall into moral compromise and sin. Most of the time, they started out very pure and innocent. They accepted the call of God on their lives and over time as their influence grew, they began to fall into deception, which again has primarily looked like separating themselves from a healthy community of believers and refusing to listen or have accountability in their lives that can provide checks and balances when necessary.

Several years ago, Dutch Sheets, an influential leader in the body of Christ, posted a letter of apology online that astounded me. With boldness and courage, he humbly addressed many of the challenges that we are facing with leaders who gain notoriety and success but have character issues. Please prayerful read his words:

> We, the leaders of the charismatic community, have operated in an extremely low level of discernment. Frankly, we often don't even try to discern. We assume a person's credibility based on gifts, charisma, the size of their ministry or church, whether they can prophesy or work a miracle, etc. (Miracles and signs are intended to validate God and His message, not the messenger; sometimes they validate the assignment of an individual, but never the person's character, lifestyle or spiritual maturity.) We leaders in the Church have become no different than the

67

world around us in our standards for measuring success and greatness.

This has contributed to the body of Christ giving millions of dollars to undeserving individuals; it has allowed people living in sin to become influential leaders—even to lead movements, allowing them influence all the way to the White House.

Through our lack of discernment we built their stages and gave them their platforms. We have been gullible beyond words—gullible leaders producing gullible sheep. When a spiritual leader we're connected with violates trust, is exposed for immorality or falls below other accepted standards of behavior, it does not exonerate us simply to say we don't condone such behavior. Those we lead trust us to let them know whom to trust. We have failed them miserably in this regard. For this lack of discernment, and for employing and passing on inappropriate standards of judgment, I repent to the Lord and ask forgiveness of the body of Christ.

A PERSONAL ENCOUNTER

At the age of 29, I had a life-changing encounter in Colorado Springs, Colorado, with Dutch Sheets at a conference where we were ministering together. For more than two hours we laughed, talked, he prophesied and prayed over me until I wept like I baby, and released a father's blessing over my life. It was refreshing beyond words. I was coming out of a serious season of rejection, and God knew what I needed and when I needed it. To close our time together, Dutch looked at me with those fiery and fatherly eyes and said the following words that I'll never forget and have written down:

Jeremiah, there are three tests that come to devour young people with influence:

1. *Lack of Character.* Many young influencers have gifting that far surpasses their character. They will never make it because they value more what they can bring to a public platform than who they are in their private living room with their wife and kids.

2. *Too Much Intellect.* Many young influencers have too much knowledge that interferes and constantly trumps what God has said to them. They lean on reason and logic alone over clear God commands and initiatives. They also believe they know everything and fail to listen to the fathers and mothers around them.

SECRETS TO STEWARDING GOD'S VOICE IN A NEW ERA

3. *Lack of Wisdom.* Many young influencers are carrying revelation and vision beyond their years of experience. They speak and people think they're 50 when really they are 30. Those who lack wisdom cannot do anything about their age so they must choose to humble themselves and focus on how to say what they've been given. They are responsible for the impression they leave upon their audience.

He then paused and stared into my eyes for what seemed like eternity and said, "I see in you that you don't lack character and you do not have too much intellect, but you are lacking in wisdom. With the revelation and vision God has given you, you have one of the most dangerous mandates in the body of Christ. Learning how to communicate and when to communicate what God has said and shown you will be your most difficult task in the days ahead. You will always be the young one in the lineup so stay humble and don't forget to ask lots of questions to those who have pioneered before you." Then he got up and walked out of the room and I sat in silence for over an hour.

LEARNING FROM SPIRITUAL PARENTS

Perhaps the greatest blessing of my life as a young influencer has been the privilege and honor of closely learning from, ministering with, and being rebuked and encouraged by so many spiritual parents in the body of Christ. Each one of them has put a deposit deep down inside me that has caused me to grow in wisdom and revelation far beyond my years.

In these precious seasons and encounters over the past 15 years, I have learned the importance of shutting up, serving them, sowing financially into their ministries, and asking questions when given the opportunity. *You will never receive from whom you will not honor.* I have watched so many young people be turned down by these spiritual parents because they are too needy and have no real fruit in their lives that is worth pruning. I have had to submit to many corrections and rebukes from them which truthfully have been very painful. I have also known what it is like for these spiritual fathers and mothers to prophesy, bless, and sow into my life in ways that has blown me away. I have never asked any of them for a dollar, platform, or favor. I have simply postured my heart to honor, serve, and obey their instructions the best I can. It's called walking in wisdom.

Each has told me the same thing in private over and over again, "Jeremiah, you have been invited into the inner circle as a young pioneer because you are actively building something and have verifiable fruit in your life, marriage, and ministry that we can see and bless." My advice to so many people who long for spiritual parenting is this:

1. Get to work building something. Stop pontif-
   icating online about the Kingdom of God and
   actually put your hand to the plow. Get some
   scars, callouses, and pay a price. True spiritual
   parents are never impressed by your gifting. They
   want to see integrity!

2. Seek to honor, serve, and sow financially into
   spiritual leaders from whom you have benefitted.
   Stop looking for free handouts and hoping they
   will share their platform with you. Be a servant
   and not an Absalom. If you have an agenda or
   dream of them fulfilling it, go ahead and repent
   now. Crucify all that fleshly ambition and walk in
   humility.

3. Be patient and do not force leadership relationships. Being overlooked is a gift that should
   cause you to wrestle internally and grow mighty
   in prayer and character. Elijah threw his cloak
   over Elisha. In other words, wait until they get
   the green light because you are finally ready now,
   not begging like an orphan for their attention and
   affection.

To anyone aspiring to become a person of influence, you
have to get some scars if you want people to respect and
listen to what you are saying. Not scars that come from a
keyboard sitting on your couch, but scars that come from
the battlefield of church planting, establishing ministries,

serving alongside pioneers, demonstrating faithfulness to a vision and spiritual authority, overcoming spiritual warfare, paying a price to see the Kingdom of God advance by force, and bearing forth real fruit! (See Matthew 11:12.)

You need real scars!

And then, you have to make sure that your scars have been properly healed by *you* going through deliverance, inner healing, and forgiveness. Vomiting on the internet about all the hell you went through in ministry is one thing—but being able to articulate your journey from a healed, delivered, and clear mind and heart is on another level.

God is inviting so many in this generation into two main realities:

1. Get offline and get on the battlefield. Stop posting all your opinions about the state of the church and start serving the church. Be quiet and learn how to love your own spouse and have a healthy marriage before you start instructing the bride of Christ on how she should act and talk. Who are you submitted to? Please stop offering online correction to the church when you don't even go to church and take correction from spiritual leaders.

2. Once you have spent years getting scars the way I just described and finally think you have something to say, then spend substantial time going

through personal deliverance, inner healing, and forgiveness. This is a totally necessary and healthy process for your emotional, mental, physical, and spiritual well-being. You must emerge and lead a generation from a mature place, not a toxic one.

A STRATEGY

If you believe that God has called you to steward influence in your generation, a clear strategy has been revealed to you that will release grace to accomplish the will of God for your life for decades to come.

1. Become part of a spiritual family where you, your marriage, and family can be loved on, accepted for who you really are, and challenged to grow. Submit to local elders and pastors who can walk with you through the challenges that life brings your way.

2. If you begin to have influence on a national and global level, you also need to seek additional accountability from more mature and seasoned leaders who have navigated success in a major way. Be in prayer about who the person or person's should be, approach them at the proper time, and share with them your heart that desires

to walk in humility and integrity before God all the days of your life.

By being involved in a healthy local church with leadership and seeking additional accountability as your influence grows, you will be taking huge steps to secure a healthy marriage and family which is most important before God.

When rejecting your need for local community and accountability, it will be only a matter of time before the seduction and pitfalls of influence will lead you down the path of moral failure, greed, and deception. By only hanging around people who see you as a celebrity, you will never walk in humility.

Keep your eyes on Jesus, pick up your cross, and follow Him. Christlikeness is always your goal as you grow in influence.

You can do it!

5

OVERCOMING JEALOUSY

Anyone who has ever done something great for God has faced the jealousy of people in their sphere of influence and even beyond. Many people are jealous of individuals they have never even met. The New Testament describes jealousy as not only a sin, but where there is jealousy, there is also every kind of evil practice (James 3:16). How sobering and alarming!

Paul told the church in Corinth, *"But even now you are not yet able, for you are still fleshly. For since there is jealousy and strife among you, are you not fleshly, and are you not walking like ordinary people?"* (1 Corinthians 3:2-3 NASB). In Galatians 5:19-21, jealousy and envy are listed as works of the flesh.

R.T. Kendall wrote, "Jealousy sometimes manifests as fear or resentment of another's success, speaking against the person, going on a vendetta to hurt their credibility, keeping them from being admired, or actually engaging in a conspiracy to destroy them."[1]

Jealousy is a very powerful and deceptive sin. It causes people to believe that everyone who has more success and influence than they do is filled with pride and arrogance.

At the heart of jealousy is anger and resentment that someone else possesses something we don't have. Jealousy is so evil and demonic that it can ultimately lead to murder as in the example of when Cain killed his brother Abel (1 John 3:12). Joseph's brothers were so jealous of the favor and love that their father Jacob had for him (Genesis 37:11) that they threw Joseph into a pit to die and later sold him into slavery.

It is impossible to grow in influence and not attract jealousy from people who are close to you and from those whom you have never even met. Some believe that if they walk in humility, no one will be jealous of them. Mark 15:10 (NLT) exposes this lie, *"For he* [Pilate] *realized by now that the leading priests had arrested Jesus out of envy."* In other words, it was the jealousy of the Pharisees and religious leaders that crucified Jesus who was the most humble Man who ever walked the earth!

NAVIGATING JEALOUSY AND MISUNDERSTANDING

It is clear then that regardless of whether someone walks in humility or not, jealousy will constantly surround those with influence. Accepting that jealousy cannot be avoided is very necessary for those called to lead.

Many people are committed to misunderstanding the words and actions of people with influence because of jealousy. In some cases, "radically committed" is more appropriate. Pioneers and leaders must accept this difficult truth in order to fulfill their destiny. Yes, we all need accountability from those who truly know us on a personal level, but I've become convinced over the years that most criticism that pioneers and leaders receive from others is actually fueled by the spirit of jealousy. The source of most of these demonic attacks comes from people's own desires to have what people of influence have.

In my book *Prophetic Pioneering,* I wrote to those with influence:

> Pioneers… You cannot fulfill the will of God without challenging the way things have always been and causing catalytic changes in the body of Christ. This will inevitably cause many to stumble, scoff, criticize, and falsely accuse you.

There is a demonic strategy set up against every pioneer in their generation that is not only aimed at destroying them, but also scattering the followers. If satan's attack is successful, everyone involved will come out of the battle hurt and wounded. Remember, satan uses people to attack, criticize, and question pioneers so that those who are getting set free, refreshed, and empowered by their life and ministry will become confused, disoriented, and altogether stop listening to the emerging pioneers.

Pioneers, you cannot allow yourself to become so easily manipulated by people's criticisms and attacks. Do not try to maintain peace in your heart and life based off of whether people accept or reject you. From my own personal experiences, most of the time God will not deliver you from your accusers, but rather He will actually save you by killing the part of you that is vulnerable to the devil by using the accusations themselves.

As a pioneer, you must recognize that both God and the devil want you to die, but for different reasons. Satan wants to destroy you through attacks and criticisms and then drain you by your unwavering need to explain yourself and your side of the story. (Please stop wasting your time and energy doing this!) On the other hand, God wants to crucify that part in you that was so easily exploited by the devil to begin with. The rest and peace that you are so desiring in your life and ministry will only come when you finally die to what people say and think about you.

Pioneers, in order to deliver you from the praise of men, God will baptize you in their criticisms and attacks. It is painful.

You will lose many friendships along the way and the misunderstandings will be many. You will pay a price that most around you will never see and not understand. You are speaking a language of reform and awakening that many in the body of Christ just don't have an eye or ear for yet. Do not grow discouraged and most of all, do not be surprised when the attacks and criticisms come. Rather than rushing to defend or explain yourself, my advice would be to go before the Lord and ask Him, "What inside of me are you exposing through the accusation and attacks of others that needs to die?"

THREE KEYS TO OVERCOME JEALOUSY

Whether you are currently walking in a measure of influence and struggling with the pain of jealousy around you,

SECRETS TO STEWARDING GOD'S VOICE IN A NEW ERA

or if you are honest and confess that you deal with jealousy and need to repent, I want to give you three keys to overcome jealousy.

1. Celebrate Others

One of the great traps of jealousy is the constant need to compete with other people rather than celebrate them. Romans 12:15 (NASB) says to *"Rejoice with those who rejoice."* As God blesses people with His favor and influence, we must learn how to rejoice with them and celebrate their success. Having this heart posture will deliver us from a jealous spirit and welcome the joy of the Lord in our lives.

2. Champion Instead of Compare

Comparison is one of the chief robbers of happiness. We must be very careful not to compare our story to the story of someone else. We have no idea what they did in private to obtain what they now have in public. God wants us to champion the people around us with encouragement to reach their unlimited potential. When we start comparing our journey with others, it begins to breed jealousy, and we start gossiping about the very people we should be learning from!

3. Accept the Call and Limitations

One of the primary ways to get freedom from jealousy is to accept the call on our lives and the limitations that come with it. Having the ability to confess what we are good at and what we are not brings so much liberty. It gives us the ability to focus on our strengths and then celebrate and champion others who are gifted in other areas that we are not as gifted. Many people must realize that their anger toward the success of others is really rooted in their anger toward God. We must humbly confess that we are just upset that He has chosen to give some a realm of influence that He has not chosen to give us.

JEALOUSY IS A PASSPORT

The greatest hostility to what God is doing *now* usually comes from those who were on the front lines of what God was doing *yesterday*. The greatest attacks on any current move of the Holy Spirit most often comes from those who were part of yesterday's move of the Spirit. The reason: JEALOUSY! For example, the breach in the relationship between King Saul and young David occurred when David began to receive praise and recognition among the people (1 Samuel 18:8). How easy it is to honor and bless others, just as long as we are still considered more influential and more loved than they are.

To those who are growing in influence and experiencing the pain and agony that comes with it, recognize that God is with you and will use these trials and tests all for His glory.

Little did David know that the years of opposition he would face from King Saul because of the anointing on his life would be his *passport* to an even greater measure of anointing when he reigned as king. The truth is that learning how to navigate jealousy in a humble way will always lead to more promotion. We must learn how to forgive and move on.

Influencers, don't be surprised if your spiritual passport is stamped full of opposition from those you once admired and even called friends. The jealousy around you is intended to be your insurance policy to stay humble and not grow arrogant over the years.

THE PROMISES OF GOD

I mentioned at the beginning of this chapter that the jealousy of Joseph's brothers landed in him in a pit to die and eventually a prison in Egypt. However, God was not finished with his story. There was a promotion waiting for Joseph that would get him into the palace where he would become second in leadership only to Pharoah. The dreams that Joseph had at age 17 of his brothers and family coming to bow down before him would come to pass decades later due to a severe famine in the land.

Imagine with me the potential anger and rage that Joseph could have had in his heart for his brothers when they finally came and saw him all those years later. This was his family! These were the very ones who should have loved him to his destiny—but rather betrayed him and left him for dead. He had spent years in a prison, was falsely accused, and must have spent so much time wondering, *God, what did I do wrong?*

Yet when given the opportunity for revenge on his brothers and having tremendous influence in Egypt, Joseph chose love and forgiveness. In his now-famous words, he told them, *"As for you, you meant evil against me, but God meant it for good in order to bring about this present result, to keep many people alive"* (Genesis 50:20 NASB).

You may have experienced terrible jealousy from your friends and family members, but you have the same opportunity now that Joseph had. Will you choose forgiveness and love toward all those who have falsely accused you, betrayed you, and slandered you? Or will you hold on to the bitterness and pain? So many with influence are afflicted with hardness of heart because they have become so accustomed to negative criticism and hateful accusations that are fueled by jealousy.

SECRETS TO STEWARDING GOD'S VOICE IN A NEW ERA

Today is the day to let it go and let God vindicate you. Release your need to defend your public reputation and allow the Holy Spirit to comfort you during this time. If God be for you, who really can be against you?

NOTE

1. R. T. Kendall, *Jealousy—The Sin No One Talks About* (Lake Mary, FL: Charisma House, 2010).

6

THE WAR BETWEEN SAUL AND DAVID

King Saul and King David were men in the Bible to whom God gave a tremendous amount of influence. Both men made mistakes while on the throne, yet only David was called, *"a man after His* [God's] *own heart"* (1 Samuel 13:14 NASB). There is so much that people of influence can learn from their mistakes and victories. For example, in young David's early years, King Saul was an orphan leader who would never become the spiritual father young David needed. Why?

1. Saul desired to COMPETE with David rather than COMMISSION him. (True spiritual leaders release young influencers once they have passed the character tests, rather than control and manipulate them.)

2. Saul cared more about his POSITION on the throne than cultivating the PRESENCE of God with David in Israel. (True spiritual leaders are servants who care more

about stewarding God's presence than they do being famous.)

3. Saul was drunk with JEALOUSY instead of JOY when David became more anointed than he was. (True spiritual leaders rejoice when their ceiling becomes the footstool of the next generation.)

Many orphan leaders with large influence are CARNI-VORES and CANNIBALS just like King Saul. They will eat (attack) their own sons and daughters when they feel threatened by their anointing and will feed on the flesh of other leaders (accuse and slander) who they see as having the potential to surpass them in grace and influence. As in the days of King Saul and young David, this same sick and twisted storyline continues to unfold within the global body of Christ. Millions are in desperate need of true spiritual parenting and sonship relationships to emerge for such a time as this. The need has never been greater!

A LIFE-CHANGING ENCOUNTER

Years ago, I attended eight revival services where thousands of people, including leaders with great influence gathered for a fresh touch of God. One night as I was observing a large altar call that took place, I suddenly had an open vision. In it, I was shown a large mountain where thousands of leaders with influence were falling on their own swords. It was a horrifying scene to be sure. The next thing I saw was a young man in a cave, crying out and weeping before the Lord. Then I heard God speak this phrase to me that I have never seen or heard before:

"I do not hear the cries that come from Mount Gilboa, but I do hear the cries that come from Engedi."

As these words began to sink into the depths of my heart, I began to cry. I knew that God was showing me where many people of influence could be headed—to Mount Gilboa where King Saul fell upon his own sword. Yet I was also filled with hope realizing that the cries from Engedi, the very place where young David humbled himself and refused to be promoted unless it be from the hand of God, would be heard.

SEVEN SIGNS INFLUENCERS ARE HEADED FOR MOUNT GILBOA

Out of this encounter with the Lord, He revealed to me that there are seven specific signs that mark the life and ministry of a leader with influence who is headed for Mount Gilboa. They are as follows:

1. Insensitivity of Heart (1 Samuel 13:5-14)

There were 30,000 chariots, 6,000 horsemen, and Philistines that outnumbered the sand on the seashore camped at Michmash against King Saul and the people of Israel. Samuel the prophet had mandated that Israel wait seven days until his arrival to offer sacrifices to the Lord before the day of battle. After seven days passed and Samuel did not arrive as scheduled, King Saul took matters into his own hands, forcing himself to offer the sacrifices, which was a violation of the law.

Upon Samuel's late arrival he said to Saul, *"You have acted foolishly; you have not kept the commandment of the Lord your God, which He commanded you, for [if you had obeyed] the Lord would have established your kingdom over Israel forever. But now your kingdom shall not endure. The Lord has sought out for Himself a man after His own heart, and the Lord has appointed him as leader and ruler over His people, because you have not kept (obeyed) what the Lord commanded you"* (1 Samuel 13:14-15 AMP).

Influential leaders headed for Mount Gilboa mistake the silence, and oftentimes vagueness of God, as a sign to take matters into their own hands, rather than an opportunity to wait and become sensitive to the Spirit of God. It was the insensitivity of the heart of Saul to the Spirit of God that cost him his kingship. God was looking for a man who would wait upon him, who would desire one thing and one thing alone, *"to gaze on the beauty of the Lord and to seek him in his temple"* (Psalm 27:4 NIV). God is looking for leaders with influence who wait for His leading and are obedient to His instructions at all costs.

2. Failing to equip others for the days ahead (1 Samuel 13:22 NASB)

"So it came about on the day of battle that neither sword nor spear was found in the hands of any of the people who were with Saul and Jonathan...."

Leaders with influence who are headed for Mount Gilboa don't know how to invest in those around them. They see influence as a means to build up their reputation and status, rather than equipping others for the work of the ministry. Influential leaders headed for Mount Gilboa are quick to silence other voices that might influence people and typically smother any move of the Spirit that they themselves did not start.

3. Building Monuments to Themselves
(1 Samuel 15:12 NIV)

"Early in the morning Samuel got up and went to meet Saul, but he was told, 'Saul has gone to Carmel. There he has set up a monument in his own honor and has turned and gone on down to Gilgal.'"

Influential leaders headed for Mount Gilboa build monuments to themselves, rather than monuments to God who enabled them to walk victoriously. These leaders obtain all their rewards upon the earth and will have little, if any, eternal rewards in Heaven. King Saul saw assignments from the Lord as nothing more than opportunities to make himself look good among the people. He was full of pride and arrogance and masked it behind being obedient to the Lord.

4. The Need to be Politically Correct
(1 Samuel 15:24 NASB)

*"Then Saul said to Samuel, 'I have sinned, for I have violated the command of the Lord and your words, because **I feared the people and listened to their voice.**'"*

King Saul was given specific instructions to slaughter the Amalekites, and all they possessed, for what they did to Israel when they were coming out of Egypt. Saul defeated the army, yet spared their King Agag and the choicest of the spoil. King Saul was so blind to his own disobedience that he was at first surprised at Samuel's anger toward his disobedience to the instruction of the Lord. As Samuel delivers a word of judgment to Saul, he finally reveals why he chose to sin; he feared the people and listened to their voice.

Influential leaders headed for Mount Gilboa believe they must be politically correct in any and all situations. Their desire to please the people around them overshadows their need to listen and obey the voice of the Lord. These leaders oftentimes believe they are walking in the will of the Lord, just as Saul did, because they have been given over to compromise and deception. They are unwilling to slaughter the "Agags" in the land. These leaders have settled for partial obedience, and they do not understand that partial obedience is no obedience at all.

5. Walking in False Humility (1 Samuel 15:30 NASB)

"Then Saul said, 'I have sinned; but please honor me now before the elders of my people and before all Israel, and go back with me, so that I may worship the Lord your God.'"

Even in King Saul's confession of his sin and arrogance, he was so full of pride that he sought to be honored among the people. Influential leaders headed for Mount Gilboa never truly repent of their sins, nor do they make it a public matter. They are full of excuses and are unwilling to submit to the process of restoration, no matter how many years that might take. The high cost of pride is the forfeit of wisdom. Those who walk in false humility will fail time and time again, until their desire to be honored, even in their failures, is uprooted and removed from their lives.

6. The Need to Have a Hand in Everything (1 Samuel 17:38 NASB)

"Then Saul clothed David with his military attire and put a bronze helmet on his head, and outfitted him with his armor."

Young David was the only man in Israel who did not fear Goliath on the day of battle. He took the giant of a man down with one stone and eventually cut off his head, yet King Saul still had a need to have his hand in the battle. Saul's attempt to clothe David in his armor was not an act of compassion or concern, this was an attempt to take credit for David's protection on the day of battle. David was wise to throw off the armor and go with what he knew would work—the leading of the Lord.

Leaders with influence headed for Mount Gilboa simply feel the need to have a hand in each and every expression of church and ministry. They demand to know every detail and expect every person to report to them at all times. Their desire to control and manipulate is stifling and exhausting to those around them. These leaders refuse to release people on the day of battle. They must have a hand in other people's successes and victories.

7. Insecurity and Unknown Identity that Fuels Jealousy (1 Samuel 18:8-9 NASB)

"Then Saul became very angry, for this lyric [saying] displeased him; and he said, 'They have given David credit for ten thousands, but to me they have given credit for only thousands! Now what more can he have but the kingdom?' And Saul eyed David with suspicion from that day on."

Influential leaders headed for Mount Gilboa look at the successes of those who are serving them as a threat to their leadership. While they voice approval and affirmation to those around them, inwardly they are filled with jealousy.

Insecurity and unknown identity are the fuel for why leaders with influence headed for Mount Gilboa do not trust others with responsibility and have the need to take credit for the victories of others.

Can you imagine if young David would have defeated Goliath wearing Saul's armor. As they cheered for David in the streets, Saul would have shouted, "Yes, but he was wearing MY armor!" King Saul was so jealous of the anointing that David walked in that he would spend the rest of his kingship pursuing David and trying to kill him, rather than pursuing the real enemies of Israel. Church leaders headed for Mount Gilboa spend more time trying to discredit and tear down ministries and people than actually engaging the real enemy, satan.

THE KINGDOM OF DAVID

The oasis of Engedi in Israel was known as a hiding place of refuge for young David and his men as he ran for his life from King Saul (1 Samuel 23:29). Although David had already been anointed as king over Israel by the prophet Samuel, he was considered a fugitive by King Saul and his men. It was in a cave in Engedi where David chose, in his words, *"not to harm the Lord's anointed"* even though he had the opportunity to kill the man who was relentlessly pursuing him for years (1 Samuel 24:10).

Ultimately, Engedi was the place where David passed a crucial test in his journey toward leading Israel: *he refused to murder King Saul and, therefore, chose not to take his destiny into his own hands.* The reason why God hears the cries that come from Engedi is because the cries from that place are ones who are ultimately surrendered to the Father's will. David even apparently had a prophetic word from the Lord that Saul would be delivered into his hands as his men reminded him, *"Behold, this is the day of which the Lord said to you, 'Behold; I am about to give your enemy over to you, and you shall do to him as it seems good to you"* (1 Samuel 24:4 NASB). David was so in tune with the Spirit of God in Engedi that he recognized that the prophetic word he received was not so that he could fulfill it by his own hands, but the prophetic word was only meant to test the deepest motives and desires of his heart! Would he take his destiny into his own hands or allow the Lord to further refine and test his heart?

SEVEN SIGNS INFLUENCERS HAVE BEEN TO ENGEDI

1. They Consistently Refuse the Temptation to Self-Promote (1 Samuel 24:17 NASB)

"And he said to David, 'You are more righteous than I; for you have dealt well with me, while I have dealt maliciously with you.'"

The very fact that David chose not to take the life of Saul when he was delivered into his hands at Engedi should speak volumes to people of influence everywhere. David recognized that it was only God Himself who could promote him, not the works of his own hands.

Influential leaders who have been to Engedi do not use ministry to promote themselves, rather they allow the Spirit of God to promote Christ within them. The problem with self-promotion is that it can only be maintained through striving, something David was not willing to do. David recognized that it was God Himself who would establish his kingship, and it would be God Himself who would sustain his kingship.

2. They Recognize That Only God Can Vindicate Them (1 Samuel 24:11 NASB)

"So, my father, look! Indeed, look at the edge of your robe in my hand! For by the fact that I cut off the edge of your robe but did not kill you, know and understand that there is no evil or rebellion in my hands, and I have not sinned against you, though you are lying in wait for my life, to take it."

It was young David who recognized that only God Himself could clear his name. Taking the life of King Saul would not do it, even though David would have been justified among the people in killing Saul. Influential leaders who have been to Engedi allow the Father to be their Defender. They do not waste time trying to clear their name or ministry. These leaders are not driven by the praise of men, but rather by the desire to see God get glory in all situations and at all times.

3. They Build Monuments to Their Nothingness (1 Samuel 24:14 NASB)

"After whom has the king of Israel gone out? Whom are you pursuing? A dead dog, a single flea?"

Influential leaders who have been to Engedi look for opportunities to humble themselves in the midst of difficult circumstances. Wouldn't it have been so easy for young David to grab King Saul in that cave and remind him, before he killed him, of how Samuel the prophet had anointed David king over Israel years before? No, David considered himself a dead dog and a single flea that King Saul was pursuing him. Those who lead and have been to Engedi do not take credit for their success and confess with Paul the apostle, *"...What do you have that you did not receive? And if you did receive it, why do you boast as if you had not received it?"* (1 Corinthians 4:7 NASB).

4. They Smell Like Sheep (1 Samuel 24:22 NASB)

"...Then Saul went to his home, but David and his men went up to the stronghold."

David was just a simple shepherd boy before Samuel anointed his head with oil and proclaimed him king over Israel. Although it would be many years before David took the throne, a shepherd's heart was being developed inside him from a very young age. David knew the importance of shepherding from within the flock, so it was natural when he began to be entrusted with a position of leadership that he knew how to lead from within his own company of men.

Influential leaders who have been to Engedi smell like sheep. They do not constantly separate themselves from those they serve. These leaders are accessible, and their lives are open books to all and any who ask.

5. They are Wilderness Trained (1 Samuel 24:8 NASB)

"And when Saul looked behind him, David bowed with his face to the ground and prostrated himself."

Here was young David, bowing down before the very man who was trying to kill him! This total act of humility and brokenness was a sheer sign that David was submitted to being wilderness trained. Influential leaders who have been to Engedi understand the difference between the "anointing" and the season of "appointing." They recognize that a "calling" is not a "commissioning." The season of Engedi is evident in the lives of church leaders who have submitted to the process of consecration. David knew the value of being wilderness trained and also realized the destruction that would come if he refused to submit to it. Leaders who have been to Engedi would rather limp into Heaven than walk straight into hell.

6. They Strengthen and Encourage Themselves in the Lord (1 Samuel 30:6 NIV)

"But David found strength himself in the Lord his God."

The day will come in every influential leader's life when there will be no encouragement, no one to offer comfort in some of the greatest times of need. Here David was at Ziklag, absolutely distraught over the Amalekites raiding the Negev where they captured his and his men's families. His own men even began talking of stoning him. David had an important decision to make as a leader. He could either give in to his own fears and give up, or he could turn to the Lord his God and strengthen Himself in who he knew God to be. It was in the wilderness of Engedi that David learned what it meant to be wholeheartedly abandoned to the Lord. Ziklag was simply another test.

Influential leaders who have been to Engedi know how to encourage themselves in the Lord. It is what separates them from the lukewarm. Church leaders who have been to Engedi carry hearts that have been tested by the praise given to them by men. In less than 24 hours from this moment in Ziklag, David would be crowned king over Israel, as Saul and his sons would fall at Mount Gilboa. Perhaps David's ability to strengthen and encourage himself in the Lord was the final test before God Himself promoted him as King.

7. They Walk in Absolute Obedience (1 Samuel 30:17 NASB)

"And David slaughtered them from the twilight until the evening of the next day; and not a man of them escaped...."

When King Saul was given the assignment to wipe out the Amalekites and everything they possessed, he made a choice to spare their King Agag and leave the choicest of the spoils for himself and his men. When David pursued the Amalekites, he slaughtered every one that he and his men could get to.

Leaders with influence who have been to Engedi complete the assignments that God has given them without delay. They understand that partial obedience is no obedience at all. David was tested in Engedi as to whether he would take matters into his own hands by killing Saul, which he refused because he was not released to do so. After inquiring of the Lord at Ziklag, David was released to pursue the Amalekites and slaughter them. Influential leaders who have been to Engedi know both when to enter into battle in obedience and when to leave the battle to the Lord in obedience.

FINAL QUESTIONS

What kind of influential leader will you choose to be? Will you follow in the footsteps of Saul in pride and arrogance or will you walk humbly before God like David?

Remember, influence is a gift that must be stewarded in an intentional and responsible way. We all make mistakes, but it is our heart posture and whether we choose to repent or grow arrogant that determines our right standing before God. David was not called a man after God's own heart because of the lack of sin in his life, but because of his brokenness and repentance over the sin in his life.

David was not called

A MAN AFTER

GOD'S OWN HEART

because of the lack of sin in his life,

but because of his

BROKENNESS and *REPENTANCE*

OVER THE SIN IN HIS LIFE.

THE DECEITFULNESS OF SIN

Why do so many people follow Jesus faithfully in obscurity but compromise their convictions when notoriety and influence comes? Hopefully this question has not only been answered throughout this book but also solutions have been offered that can guide men and women of influence to decades of success both in private and public.

Whether God has gifted someone with influence over hundreds or influence with tens of thousands, the fallen nature of humanity constantly seeks to trap as many victims as it possibly can. It would be very beneficial for us all to be reminded about just how deadly sin really is, how powerful the blood of Jesus is, and learn from several key Bible stories so we can be empowered to walk in truth and light.

Sin will take us further than we want to go, it will make us pay a price we do not want to pay, and it will keep us longer than we want to stay. It was in the Garden of Eden where satan the serpent deceived Eve into eating from the tree of the knowledge of good and evil, which God had forbidden.

Her choice to sin—or rather to act independently of God to pursue her own selfish desires—caused a death sentence to be pronounced over humanity that could not be broken until centuries later when Jesus Christ shed His blood at Calvary. Isaiah the prophet said it like this, *"But your iniquities* [sins] *have separated you from God..."* (Isaiah 59:2 NIV). Indeed, God did not plan their fall, but He did plan for it.

THE CONSEQUENCES OF SIN

After Adam and Eve had sinned against God in the Garden of Eden, He approached them.

> *Now they heard the sound of the Lord God walking in the garden in the cool of the day, and the man and his wife hid themselves from the presence of the Lord God among the trees of the garden. Then the Lord God called to the man, and said to him, "Where are you?" He said, "I heard the sound of You in the garden, and I was afraid because I was naked; so I hid myself." And He said, "Who told you that you were naked?*

*Have you eaten from the tree from which I com-
manded you not to eat?" The man said, "The
woman whom You gave to be with me, she gave
me some of the fruit of the tree, and I ate." Then
the Lord God said to the woman, "What is this
that you have done?" And the woman said, "The
serpent deceived me, and I ate"* (Genesis 3:8-13
NASB).

Just one chapter earlier, Adam and Eve had walked with
God in the Garden of Eden without any fear, any shame, or
even awareness that they were naked. But their choice to sin
had opened an evil pandora's box that has forever plagued
humanity. True pleasure was found in the presence of their
Creator. They were designed for intimacy with Him. They
had unlimited and unhindered access to the God of the
universe. Unfortunately, Adam and Eve had now discovered that sinning was not the gaining of pleasure as satan
had deceived them into thinking, but rather sinning was
the loss of true pleasure.

We see very clearly in these verses the consequences of
sin that entered the human race as a result of Adam and
Eve's choice to sin and rebel against God. They are fear,
shame, and contempt. Let's look more closely at each of
them.

When God called to Adam, he said, *"When I heard you,
I was afraid because I was naked; **so I hid myself.**"* Prior to

SECRETS TO STEWARDING GOD'S VOICE IN A NEW ERA

them sinning, there is no record of them ever being afraid of God or feeling the need to hide themselves from Him. It is only when they chose to sin that the consequences of sin began their destructive work.

Where does fear come from? Certainly not from God! Fear was born in the Garden of Eden because of humanity's choice to reject perfect love and union with their Father. Fear was a result of choosing disobedience. The Scriptures are clear, *"God has not given us a spirit of fear and timidity, but of love, power, and self-discipline* [a sound mind]" (2 Timothy 1:7 NLT).

And what about shame? The Scripture says that Adam and Eve hid from God because they realized they were naked. Shame is the fear of being exposed. Being exposed is connected to the fear of being rejected and abandoned. In their nakedness was their shame. It is the story of humankind!

When God confronts Adam about their sin, listen to his response, *"The man replied, 'It was **the woman you gave me** who gave me the fruit, and I ate it'"* (Genesis 3:12 NLT). Read that again very carefully. Rather than Adam taking responsibility for his choice to sin, he condemns both Eve and God for his bad choice. His language of "The woman" and "you gave me" reveal his attempt to blame both Eve and God for his rebellion and sin. Failure to accept responsibility for our sin and failure is the source of all pride. From

FAILURE TO ACCEPT

RESPONSIBILITY

for our *sin* and *FAILURE*

is the source of

ALL PRIDE.

the Fall in the Garden of Eden, humanity has always been blaming someone else for their sin and failures.

These are three primary consequences of sin that we have now discovered in the fall of humanity in Genesis 3. The deceitfulness of sin has always been about making it look and feel like rebellion against God is gaining pleasure, when the truth is that rebellion means losing life's pleasure. Fear, shame, and contempt are the evil trifecta that seek to keep humanity away from intimacy and union with God.

As destructive and evil as sin really was and is, God provided His only Son Jesus to break the death sentence over humanity of eternal death. Galatians 3:13 (NASB) says, *"Christ redeemed us from the curse of the Law, having become the curse for us..."* and *"For God made Christ, who never sinned, to be the offering for our sin, so that we could be made right with God through Christ"* (2 Corinthians 5:21 NLT).

THE FREEDOM OF CHRIST

What Adam and Eve could not overcome in the Garden of Eden, Jesus Christ overcame in the Garden of Gethsemane. Adam and Eve disobeyed, choosing their own will and way. Jesus Christ was obedient to the Father as He said, *"not My will, but Yours be done"* (Luke 22:42 NASB). Adam and Eve experienced the consequences of sin as fear, shame, and contempt gripped the core of their being. Jesus Christ experienced victory over sin as He nailed it to the Cross. With His resurrection, Jesus made a way for sin to be conquered forever. Colossians 1:13-14 (NASB) says, *"For He rescued us from the domain of darkness, and transferred us to the kingdom of His beloved Son, in whom we have redemption, the forgiveness of sin."*

Paul wrote in Romans 6:12-14 (NASB):

> *Therefore sin is not to reign in your mortal body so that you obey its lusts, and do not go on presenting the parts of your body to sin as instruments of unrighteousness; but present yourselves to God as those who are alive from the dead, and your body's parts as instruments of righteousness for God. For sin shall not be master over you, for you are not under the Law but under grace.*

Living a lifestyle free from sin is possible because of the precious blood of Jesus that was shed at Calvary. Our old ways of rebellion and independence have been crucified with Jesus, and we have truly been made new in Him. We have not only been granted eternal life, but we can now walk in freedom over fear, shame, and contempt.

WRONG THINKING IS TOXIC

One of the greatest challenges to walking in victory over sin and its consequences as people of influence is actually believing the lies that it is not possible! Isn't that just shocking? The truth is that nowhere in the New Testament are Christians ever referred to as "sinners." Quite the opposite! Those who have put their faith in Jesus Christ are actually referred to as "saints" because Christians now have a new nature and have the privilege of walking with the Holy Spirit who leads and guides us into all truth. This is why 2 Corinthians 5:17 (NLT) says that, *"anyone who belongs to Christ has become a new person. The old life is gone; a new life has begun!"*

There is a very disturbing ideology permeating the global Church today that has deceived many into thinking that adultery, drunkenness, abuse, and so many other sins are not only acceptable but just part of being a Christian. This wrong thinking concerning sin and rebellion is not only toxic, but it is leading millions to hell. It is a direct assault on the blood that Jesus Christ shed and denies the power of His resurrection.

Sin is no longer our master because we now walk in the grace that God has provided for each of us in His Son. Grace is not a license to sin—it is divine influence upon our hearts that grants us the empowerment to walk in godliness and righteousness (Titus 2:11-12).

GOD HATED SIN SO MUCH

that He would rather see

His Son Jesus Die

THAN TO SEE sin live!

We have to understand that God hated sin so much that He would rather see His Son Jesus die than sin live! Ponder that truth for a moment please. Steve Hill said, "Treating sin casually makes you a casualty." If we are going to see a generation of men and women walk with influence for decades in the body of Christ and uphold a standard of righteousness, we have to continually sound the alarm on the deceitfulness of sin. The love of money, seeking the fame and applause of people, and moral compromise in our Christian values all lead down a destructive path that we can reject if we choose to truly follow Jesus. It is possible, like Daniel and even Joseph, to walk in great influence in our nations and yet still maintain integrity and the fear of the Lord. However, it all starts with recognizing just how deceitful sin is and the painful consequences that come with wrong choices.

PERVERSION AND SIN

I believe that a generation of influencers is emerging who recognize the power we have been given as Christians over wickedness and sin because of the blood of Jesus. As our sphere of influence grows and temptation comes knocking on our doors, we do have the ability to submit to God, resist the devil, and he will flee! (See James 4:7.) We must not entertain any false grace messages that seek to normalize wickedness and sin in the life of a Christian and especially a leader. We should categorically reject this deception and fix our eyes on Jesus.

The story is told in 1 Kings 16:29-34 (NASB) about an evil king named Ahab:

*Now Ahab the son of Omri became king over Israel in the thirty-eighth year of Asa king of Judah, and Ahab the son of Omri reigned over Israel in Samaria for twenty-two years. Ahab the son of Omri did evil in the sight of the Lord more than all who were before him. And as though **it had been a trivial thing for him to walk in the sins** of Jeroboam the son of Nebat, **he married Jezebel** the daughter of Ethbaal king of the Sidonians, and went and **served Baal, and worshiped him**. So he erected an altar for Baal at the house of Baal, which he built in Samaria. Ahab also made the Asherah. So Ahab did more to provoke the Lord God of Israel to anger than all the kings of Israel who were before him. In his days Hiel the Bethelite rebuilt Jericho; he laid its foundations with the loss of Abiram his firstborn, and set up its gates with the loss of his youngest son Segub, in accordance with the word of the Lord, which He spoke by Joshua the son of Nun.*

The first very important thing to note in this passage is Ahab's approach to sin. Rather than recognize the deceitfulness of it, he invites it into his life and reaps destructive consequences. It says, *"it had been a **trivial** thing for him to walk in the sins..."* The word *trivial* means, "of little value, importance, or worth." In other words, King Ahab did not think it was a big deal to walk in the sins of his fathers.

What happens next? The Scriptures say that Ahab married Jezebel, an evil pagan woman full of immorality and wickedness. Please now carefully consider how the deceitfulness of sin really works.

A trivial approach to sin produces unrighteous affections so that we become attracted to people and things that we were never meant to become attracted to. If Ahab would have operated with a correct view on sin, which would have looked like denouncing it and turning away, he would have never married Jezebel. However, because his approach to sin was passive, it opened the door to the spirit of perversion in his life—and it cost him dearly.

Think about how many people lie to themselves about watching pornography, for example. "It's only an image on a screen" they say. What they fail to realize is that by watching pornography, they are actually fellowshipping with demons and opening their entire home, marriage, and family to the works of the devil. Over time, they become addicted and attracted to people and acts that God never intended for them to entertain.

A trivial approach to sin

PRODUCES

UNRIGHTEOUS AFFECTIONS

so that we become *ATTRACTED*

TO PEOPLE AND THINGS

THAT WE WERE NEVER MEANT

to become attracted to.

Others say, "It's only one drink of alcohol or only one hit of a drug." Are you clearly seeing how deceitful sin is? It's like Adam and Eve in the Garden of Eden all over again. "Come on," satan whispers, "It's only a little taste, it's only a little pleasure, God will forgive you."

I sense that the Holy Spirit is currently bringing conviction to many who are reading this right now. Is there hidden compromise in your life as you navigate influence? Are you being pressured to forsake Christian values for worldly standards? The Bible says, *"the little foxes that ruin the vineyards"* (Song of Solomon 2:15 NIV). In other words, a little compromise here and a little compromise there eventually lead to full-blown deception and a lifestyle that is not pleasing to God. *We must not allow a foothold to turn into a stronghold!*

I want you to hear me clearly: You can become a man and woman of God with great influence who refuses to compromise with sin. Jesus did it and so can we. He made a way to walk in absolute freedom and integrity with His death and resurrection. By His grace, we can steward wealth without falling in love with it.

We can influence thousands but recognize God gave us the platform so we can lift *Him* up, not ourselves. Don't miss this divine moment to search your heart and repent of any known sin in your life. Seek deliverance from demonic strongholds if you have to. Ask the Holy Spirit to reveal any lies you have believed about sin and replace it with the truth that is found in God's Word.

BREAKING GENERATIONAL CURSES

Another powerful story in the Bible that demonstrates the deceitfulness of sin is found in Genesis 9:18-25 (NASB):

Now the sons of Noah who came out of the ark were Shem, Ham, and Japheth; and Ham was the father of Canaan. These three were the sons of Noah, and from these the whole earth was populated. Then Noah began farming and planted a vineyard. He drank some of the wine and became drunk, and uncovered himself inside his tent. Ham, the father of Canaan, saw the nakedness of his father, and told his two brothers outside. But Shem and Japheth took a garment and laid it on both their shoulders and walked backward and covered the nakedness of their father; and their faces were turned away, so that they did not see their father's nakedness. When Noah awoke from his wine, he knew what his youngest son had done to him. So he said "Cursed be Canaan; a servant of servants he shall be to his brothers."

Because Noah got drunk, he gave one of his sons, Ham, permission to see something he should have never seen if Noah would have stayed sober. Again, I want to be a voice of clarity here when it comes to the deceitfulness of sin. When the choice to sin becomes "not a big deal," it exposes marriages, families, and individuals to perversion and wickedness that they never had to experience if we would just walk in obedience to Jesus and the fear of God.

The story says that, *"Ham, the father of Canaan **saw** the nakedness of his father...."* There is a debate among scholars regarding the motive and intent behind Ham seeing his father naked. In fact, many of them believe that there is great possibility that Ham actually enjoyed his father's nakedness. In other words, there was a spirit of perversion resting upon him. This makes much more sense when you consider Noah waking up and the curse he places not on his son, Ham, but on his grandson Canaan! What other explanation is there due to the severity of the judgment that Noah released?

The tragic truth in this story is that one generation's compromise led to the next generations captivity. Noah's choice to get drunk opened the door of perversion to Ham, which resulted in a generational curse being placed on Canaan!

When will men and women of influence realize that satan is not just after tempting us into sin, he wants to destroy our marriages, family, and all those who follow us as well!

SHE UNDRESSED

I know a minister who was counseling a woman through a divorce. It was messy and he had a lot of compassion for what she was going through. As time went on, they started developing an unhealthy emotional bond. At their scheduled appointment one night, the woman got up and asked to use the restroom. When she returned, she was undressed and ask the minister if he would have sex with her.

Startled and immediately recognizing the trap of the devil, he asked her to please go put her clothes on. She did and returned. He told her that they could no longer meet, then asked if he could show her something. The minister pulled out his wallet and took out a picture of him and his wife and a picture of him and his kids. He then took a lighter off his desk and burned both pictures. He told the woman, "If I would have committed adultery with you, I would have destroyed my marriage and family just like burning those two photos." What appears to be temporary pleasure oftentimes carries with it devastating consequences.

This very real and terrible story illustrates just how seductive and deceitful sin really is. It's always more than just one look, one taste, or even one touch. Sin is deadly. It destroys marriages, families, and individuals.

THE GOOD NEWS

Although wickedness and sin is constantly seeking to destroy men and women with influence, God always has an answer for compromise in every generation. While Ahab and Jezebel operated in demonic power over a nation, God raised up a man of covenant named Elijah! Elijah was anointed with a mandate for restoration and revival. He was uncompromising in his convictions and a true prophet of God.

Noah placed a curse on his grandson Canaan due to drunkenness and perversion. Compromise ruled the land until God raised up a covenant man named Abram! When God gave Abraham the land of Canaan, it was more than a place of real estate! It was reversing a generational curse that Noah had put on his grandson Canaan.

The hour is late in the nations. The need for men and women of influence who walk with God and hate wickedness and sin has never been greater. Our choices to walk in righteousness and integrity will bring about generational blessing that will touch thousands one day. Our desire to walk humbly and justly before God and give Him all the credit for any and all success we have will keep our pride and ego in check.

The choice is ours. Will we be influencers who walk in compromise with the world—or will be influencers who walk in covenant with God?

UPROOTING THE SPIRIT OF REJECTION

Those who walk in any realm of influence have all faced rejection. In fact, it is quite normal to be rejected and accepted by different groups of people all at the same time as someone fulfills their God-given destiny. Whenever a person begins to experience the favor and promotion of God on their life, it can become very difficult to determine who is for them and who is against them. Take Daniel for example.

The Bible says that Daniel began to distinguish himself among other leaders because he possessed an extraordinary spirit. As he walked in this special grace and anointing, it caused a spirit of false accusation and jealousy to rise up against him through other leaders. However, he was honored and accepted by King Darius.

What had Daniel done wrong to face such rejection and opposition by his peers? Absolutely nothing! The spiritual warfare that Daniel faced was so great that he ended up being thrown into a lion's den—but God protected him and spared his life as he went through a very difficult season of rejection that sought to take even his life (Daniel 6).

THE HALL OF FAME

A quick read throughout Scripture reveals that the men and women who have chosen to follow God have always gone through difficult seasons of rejection:

- Israel constantly complained against the leadership of Moses and rejected him.

- Jeremiah was called a traitor by the people and lowered into a mud-filled cistern.

- David was told he was too weak and young to fight Goliath.

- Joseph was rejected by his family, thrown in a pit and left to die, and was later sold into slavery and spent time in prison.

- All of the twelve disciples, except John, were martyred for their faith.

Perhaps no one faced greater rejection than Jesus Christ:

He was despised and rejected—a man of sorrows, acquainted with deepest grief. We turned our backs on him and looked the other way (Isaiah 53:3 NLT).

He was in the world, and though the world was made through him, the world did not recognize him. He came to that which was his own, but his own did not receive him. (John 1:10-11 NIV).

In order to do the will of God, we must accept that we will be rejected by people. It is impossible to please God without facing human opposition. In the words of Leonard Ravenhill, "To be right with God has often meant to be in trouble with men." However, we do have the choice to not walk in a spirit of rejection. When the spirit of rejection is operating in someone's life, they constantly see themselves through the lens of a victim. Their heart becomes hardened over time because of the hurtful words spoken against them. When this happens, bitterness, unforgiveness, and anger begin operating in someone who operates out of a rejection.

THE SPIRIT OF REJECTION

The following are five questions we can ask ourselves to help determine whether we need the spirit of rejection uprooted from our lives:

1. Am I easily offended?

People who operate out of a spirit of rejection anticipate and expect negative and hurtful responses from others.

2. When I am questioned, do I become agitated or angry?

Through the eyes of rejection, normal interaction and questions are interpreted as personal attacks. People who operate out of a spirit of rejection are constantly suspicious of the motives and intentions of people's hearts toward them.

3. Do I need to be considered an expert on everything?

Past experiences of rejection that are not addressed and healed will wrongly lead people to believe that they have to know it all, because anything they don't know is perceived as intellectual weakness.

4. Do I experience marked mood swings?

Constant rejection and the fear of it leads people to allow their emotions to lead their lives. They will go from happy to sad and calm to angry based on their perceptions of whether people like them or not. This is toxic behavior that must be uprooted through forgiveness and deliverance.

5. Do I do things to merely gain acceptance and attention?

People who operate out of a spirit of rejection consistently feel the need to perform in order to win the approval of their family and friends.

It is very important that we separate the rejection that we all face as we grow in influence from the spirit of rejection that is demonic and seeks to trap us in bitterness,

unforgiveness, and overwhelming feelings of abandon-
ment. The difference between the two is found in not only
how we choose to respond when we are rejected by others,
but also in recognizing where our true source of acceptance
must come from to begin with.

THE EXAMPLE OF JESUS CHRIST

Jesus Christ faced so much rejection and opposition, yet He
never avoided anyone because of a wounded and offended
heart.

Jesus Christ never responded in anger and didn't act like
a victim because of all the rejection He faced.

How could Jesus walk through rejection so ably? Let's
start in John 2:23-25 (NLT) to find out:

> Because of the miraculous signs Jesus did in Jeru-
> salem at the Passover celebration, many began to
> trust in him. But Jesus didn't trust them, because
> he knew all about people. No one needed to tell
> him about human nature, for he knew what was
> in each person's heart.

Did you catch that? Jesus didn't trust them because
He knew what was in their hearts! In other words, Jesus

knew that He could never find the source of true acceptance from another human being. It was impossible. The longing for and true acceptance only comes from God the Father.

This is why one man wisely said, "If you live for the praise of men, you will die by their criticisms." The human heart really is fickle. One day they loved Jesus because of the miracles He performed, and the next day they wanted to kill Him because of the truth He spoke to them.

Jesus Christ faced so much rejection and yet He didn't operate in a spirit of rejection because He knew where His true Source of acceptance came from—God the Father. As influencers, we must recognize the danger of craving the approval and applause of other people. Fame and fortune may come and go but what God says about us must be our focus. The crowds shouted about Jesus, "Hosanna!" one day and "Crucify Him!" the next.

I do not believe the Scriptures say that Jesus did not trust humans. Rather, He walked with realistic expectations about them. If we are ever going to fully uproot the spirit of rejection from our lives, we have to accept that most of our expectations we have for people, including our spouses and children, are unrealistic. We are guilty of desiring to put people in a position that is only reserved for God. Only He can satisfy and meet the longings of our heart to be known, loved, and accepted.

Yes, we should all have as many deep friendships and relationships with human beings as possible; however, we cannot solely depend upon their words and actions to determine our well-being.

DEALING WITH FALSE ACCUSATION

Knowing in an experiential way that we are truly loved and accepted by God will deliver us from any spirit of rejection that tries to attach itself to us when people reject us. We can choose to forgive and not harbor bitterness and anger toward family and friends when they reject us, because we understand that they are human and therefore flawed. The only One who will never forsake or abandon us is God (Hebrews 13:5).

Going through rejection for various reasons is difficult; however, I have found that being rejected because of false accusation is extremely painful and hurtful. It's one thing if people don't like certain things about our speech, personality, or actions and choose to not engage with us, but it's entirely different when people reject us because of lies, gossip, and false slander.

How do we deal with false accusation and not allow the lies and false reporting to cause us to operate in a spirit of rejection? Let's read 1 Peter 2:22-23 (NASB):

He [Jesus] *who committed no sin, nor was any deceit found in His mouth; and while being abusively insulted, He did not insult in return; while suffering, He did not threaten, but kept entrusting Himself to Him who judges righteously.*

Can you imagine all the false accusation and slander that Jesus went through in His life and ministry and yet was without sin? (See 2 Corinthians 5:21.) He was perfectly innocent, yet they mocked, beat, and crucified Him on a tree. He walked in all humility, yet because of jealousy and envy they killed Him (Mark 15:10).

How did Jesus Christ overcome false accusation and not allow Himself to operate out of a spirit of rejection? He kept entrusting Himself to His Father who judges righteously. God knowing the truth about Him was enough for Jesus. In prayer one day meditating on this reality, I broke down crying thinking about my own vindictive desires to clear my name over false accusations that had been spoken against me. I wanted to set the record straight online about who I was and the ministry God had given me. The Holy Spirit whispered to me, *"He was led like a sheep to the slaughter, and like a lamb before its shearer is silent, so He did not open His mouth"* (see Isaiah 53:7).

I'm so grateful for the example that Jesus Christ, the greatest Influencer of all time, has left us as His followers. No one faced a more demonic onslaught of attack and rejection, yet He walked in the power of love and forgiveness. Jesus refused to allow the spirit of rejection to take root in His heart by living out two main realities:

1. He knew where His true Source of acceptance came from and had realistic expectations regarding human beings. He knew their faults and failures and refused to give them the place in His heart that was reserved only for the Father.

2. When faced with false accusation, lies, and slander, He entrusted Himself to the Father who judges justly. God knowing the truth about who Jesus was set Him free from the need to defend Himself or set the record straight with His accusers.

The thoughts and ways of Jesus Christ are higher than ours. Through His life, death, and resurrection, He offers freedom today from the spirit of rejection. It's time to heal, forgive, and fall more in love with Him than ever before. May His words in Matthew 5:43-48 (NASB) have the final say over our lives:

> You have heard that it was said, "You shall love your neighbor and hate your enemy." But I say to you, love your enemies and pray for those who persecute you, so that you may prove yourselves to be sons of your Father who is in heaven; for He causes His sun to rise on the evil and the good,

and sends rain on the righteous and the unrighteous. For if you love those who love you, what reward do you have? Even the tax collectors, do they not do the same? And if you greet only your brothers and sisters, what more are you doing than others? Even the Gentiles, do they not do the same? Therefore you shall be perfect, as your heavenly Father is perfect.

4

NAVIGATING SPIRITUAL WARFARE

I have never met anyone who has significant influence who has not gone through serious spiritual warfare on multiple occasions in their lives. Ephesians 6:12 (NIV) says, *"For our struggle is not against flesh and blood, but against the rulers, against the authorities, against the powers of this dark world and against the spiritual forces of evil in the heavenly realms."* We all make personal mistakes and human beings can even oppose us at times, but there is also a real unseen enemy of our souls named the devil, who loves to work through people and situations to distract and destroy us.

In Revelation 12, a scene unfolds where a woman is in labor, but the devil is standing on guard, seeking to devour her child. Whenever God is about to birth something great in a generation, satan is always looking to kill, steal, and destroy (John 10:10). Think about Moses! God brought forth a mighty deliverer in Egypt, yet Pharoah had proclaimed a death decree over all the firstborn children of the Hebrews (Exodus 1:15-22). By miraculous intervention, Moses was spared and satan's plans were thwarted.

What about the birth of Christ? Herod had decreed that again, all the firstborn Hebrew children were to be slaughtered. Through a warning dream given to Joseph, the life of Christ was spared even as a baby (Matthew 2:16-18).

Intense spiritual warfare most often comes in two primary seasons:

1. Seasons of birthing

2. Seasons of transition

Jesus walked the earth for 30 years, and as He transitioned into His three-and-a-half year ministry, satan met Him in the wilderness during a 40-day fast to tempt Him. After being unsuccessful, the Scriptures says that *"He [satan]...left Him until a more opportune time"* (Luke 4:13 AMP). In other words, satan is always looking to attack and strike in strategic seasons of our lives, especially when we are vulnerable. New seasons and transitional seasons are often specifically marked by unknowns where we are navigating relationships, geographic shifts, and more. This is why 1 Peter 5:8 (NASB) says, *"Be of sober spirit, be on the alert. Your adversary, the devil, prowls around like a roaring lion, seeking someone to devour."*

NAVIGATING SPIRITUAL WARFARE

I have had the privilege of traveling and doing ministry worldwide. I and our teams have cast out many demons from people as well as dealt with spiritual strongholds over certain countries and regions of the United States. However, the strongest spiritual warfare I have ever faced is when I have planted churches. There is something about birthing and establishing the work of God in a specific city or region long term that causes satan and his demons to stir up spiritual warfare on unprecedented levels. I encourage you to read a book I wrote, titled *The Warrior Bride*, regarding spiritual warfare in much more depth.

THE FIVE CANCERS

I had a prophetic dream one night where God showed me that there was a specific cancer or demonic attack assigned to each of the five ministries mentioned in Ephesians 4:11-16. The revelation and prophetic insight I received has been extremely beneficial in navigating spiritual warfare in my own life and the lives of many in the body of Christ. The following is what I saw in the dream:

1. Apostles - **Leviathan Attack**

2. Prophets - **Jezebel Spirit Attack**

3. Teachers - **Religious Spirit Attack**

4. Pastors - **Discouragement Attack**

5. Evangelists - **Vanity Attack**

Apostles and Leviathan Attack

I mentioned earlier that the strongest demonic attacks I have endured in my life are when I have planted churches. Planting churches is an apostolic function, so a severe leviathan attack came to destroy the work that God was calling us to establish. There are many apostles in the body of Christ right now whom God is calling to birth new works and establish churches that must be warned about the leviathan spirit.

Many times, leviathan will appear in dreams and visions as an alligator or crocodile. Leviathan is called the "crooked serpent" in the book of Isaiah or "twister." The nature of this evil spirit is described in Isaiah 27:1 and Job 41. In Job 41:34 (KJV), it is described as, *"king over all the children of pride"* and it is pride that gives this demonic spirit access into people's lives. Was it not satan coming as a crooked serpent, full of pride, who sought to twist the words that God had spoken to Adam and Eve?

Leviathan brings false accusation against people, especially those in leadership positions. When apostles birth and plant churches in cities and regions, leviathan will work through prideful leaders and people in order to attack the new thing God desires to do. When God is calling people to transition geographically or when church leadership is transitioning into what God has for them, the spirit of leviathan will operate through pride to bring forth false accusation, twist people's words, and bring division. "I did not say that," and, "Yes, you did," and, "I know what you're doing," and, "What are you talking about" are common phrases that come up when the spirit of leviathan is at work.

Leviathan is an enemy moving below or behind the scenes to ruin a person's life, to devour with words that bite, and to drag their victim down into a death roll—just like an alligator would. Leviathan attacks bring slander, gossip, and verbal abuse. This evil spirit operates through deceitful people in authority who work undercover to destroy with biting words of accusation.

It is very important to remember that the leviathan spirit comes to twist people's words and call their motives and intentions into question. It brings forth false accusation, slander, and gossip. Church leaders and people who are prideful will attack anyone God has called to birth a new thing or who are trying to transition into their next season. Those who operate in leviathan will stay quiet behind the scenes as they gather information about people and churches. Over time, they will begin to come up with their own narratives that are full of false accusation and lies. Those who operate in leviathan attract liars and bitter people who are harboring unforgiveness.

I have seen firsthand the leviathan spirit ruin the relationships and friendships that people have had for years! For example, God calls someone to move into a new season, to birth something, and all of a sudden the words, motives, and intentions of everyone's hearts are questioned and false accusations, lies, and slanders are next. Satan has a foothold through pride, and it will eventually become a stronghold if we do not recognize and rebuke this evil spirit at work.

Whenever we stop believing the best about someone, we must seek to build relationship and discover the truth. Waiting months and years to forgive and gain clarity over our concerns opens the door to leviathan. Beware!

Overcoming Leviathan

Why is pride the foundation of false accusation? Because false accusation elevates itself over another person and the truth in order to become judge, jury, and executioner. The evil spirit of leviathan can attack anyone, but it will specifically target apostles as they plant and birth new works. It will call their words, motives, and intentions into question. It will spread lies and false accusation in their region and city in order to prevent people from receiving from their God-given influence.

How does someone overcome leviathan? What do you do when people have believed lies about you and are spreading gossip and slander? We follow the example of Jesus and walk in humility, integrity, and forgiveness. The only way to defeat the prideful and accusatory spirit of leviathan is to not retaliate in pride and accusation ourselves. We must go low, stay humble, and allow Jesus to defend us. This is incredibly difficult, but entrusting ourselves to God and the fact that He knows the truth will give us the grace we need to remain humble and keep advancing the Kingdom of God. As James 4:6 (NLT) says, *"God opposes the proud but gives grace to the humble."*

Prophets and Jezebel Attack

The enemy of the prophetic is the Jezebel spirit. While this evil spirit can attack anyone, Jezebel specifically targets those who dare to speak for God and will do anything in its power to silence and shut down what the Holy Spirit wants to do and say. Jezebel was an evil woman in the Old Testament (1 Kings 16) and in the New Testament (Revelation 2).

Jezebel is a demonic spirit at work in the modern-day Church that has a very specific assignment to keep people from hearing and obeying God. The Jezebel spirit is gender neutral. It operates through men and women. When you say "Jezebel spirit," people typically think that it is a woman who has a leadership gift on her life and when she starts exercising it, she's a "Jezebel." I want to tell you categorically that this is not true and oftentimes comes from individuals who struggle with insecurity and jealousy.

I have cast out the Jezebel spirit of both men and women. I've expelled it out of church leaders. How do I know that it is this spirit? Because on numerous occasions when asking the demon its name, it says, "I am Jezebel." When engaging in deliverance ministry, it's important that we separate the spirit at work from the person who is being tormented.

The Jezebel spirit uses manipulation. It uses control. It manifests through flattery, seduction, intimidation, immorality, and trickery to seek its own will and way. It operates best in truces and treaties because it hates the truth of God's word meant to set it free. The Jezebel spirit needs a host to partner with it. This is why King Ahab, who was a passive leader, was the ideal partner for Jezebel. The Jezebel loves tormenting leaders and people who are non-confrontational. The goal of this evil spirit is to oppress and dominate its victims into submission and toleration. Prophets and Christians who operate within boundaries and refuse to be manipulated and controlled infuriate the Jezebel spirit.

The length of time that the spirit of Jezebel has operated in and through an individual will oftentimes determine whether the spirit is immature or mature. For example, an immature Jezebel spirit will manifest in relationships fairly quickly, fast enough so that the potential damage it can bring will be minimized. Control, manipulation, fear, emotionalism, and seduction (to name a few tactics) will be detected almost immediately with an immature Jezebel spirit at work. On the other hand, a mature Jezebel spirit will be very calculated in its approach and relationships. At times, it will take weeks, months, and sometimes years to manifest. Beware, it is plotting, planning, and will not just go away with time.

A mature Jezebel spirit draws its strength from individuals who have come under its influence over time and spins an evil web of confusion around its victims. The strategy is to build an army so that when Jezebel takes out leaders and individuals, its actions are justified by a majority, not a minority, so it doesn't seem divisive or suspicious.

The spirit of Jezebel is fueled by sympathizers. It loves throwing "woe is me" parties. It attempts to gain an audience with anyone it can find, especially those in authority. Jezebel is magnetically attracted to individuals who are non-confrontational. If you are called as a prophet or as a believer who operates in prophecy, be on guard against the Jezebel spirit and know that it will oftentimes target you and the influence God has given you.

Overcoming Jezebel Attack

When you find yourself dealing with an *immature* Jezebel spirit, confront it immediately and call for repentance. Many people do not realize they are operating under its influence. When you find yourself dealing with a *mature* Jezebel spirit, all hands on deck! You are not facing just the person it's operating through, you are about to deal with all of its minions too! This spirit has most likely already preyed upon all the young people who have looked for a spiritual mom or dad, and they will choose sides—and it won't be yours.

Take courage, greater is He who is in you, than this evil spirit you are dealing with. You must fight for freedom and not allow this spirit to work any longer. In most cases, completely breaking ties with the person who has partnered with the Jezebel spirit is necessary, no matter what kind of influence it has. Better to be free and have breath than enslaved and suffocated.

Teachers and Religious Spirit Attack

God has given His Church fivefold teachers who instruct the saints on how to study and obey the Word of God. However, when the religious spirit starts attacking teachers of God's Word, they weaponize the Bible against people and become legalistic, hard, and rigid. Oftentimes, they lose compassion for the hurting and broken and become angry and disillusioned over the sin in the Church. There is a way in which a teacher can minister the Word of God with truth and integrity and allow the Holy Spirit to bring conviction and transformation.

However, there is also a demonic way in which a teacher can minister the Word of God out of a religious spirit and the fruit of it will become a yoke of bondage and slavery among the hearers. Teaching lawlessness is dangerous, but so is teaching legalism. The only path God has called us to walk on as believers is the path of life in the Holy Spirit. Both lawlessness and legalism are extremes that have brought tremendous damage to the body of Christ. When the religious spirit attacks and attaches itself to teachers, they become obsessed with certain doctrines and will not allow other perspective or prophetic insight.

The religious spirit has a form of godliness but denies its power (2 Timothy 3:5). It seeks to tame, domesticate, constrain, and cripple Christians who pursue the deeper things of God. The religious spirit is the author of cessationism, a doctrine of demons that says the gifts of the Holy Spirit ceased with the Apostolic Age. It dismisses one member of the Trinity, denies the inerrancy of Scripture, discredits the mystery of God, and doesn't allow followers of Jesus to move from the Cross to Pentecost. It traps Christians in religious routine and invites them into performance and hypocrisy. The religious spirit acts as a gatekeeper for many other demons: it gets in the door and then invites all its friends. This is why so many Western churches have become demon daycares.

Overcoming Religious Spirit Attack

Walking with the Holy Spirit as our greatest Teacher and trusting Him to lead and guide us into the truth will deliver teachers from operating in a religious spirit or even being attacked by it. If you are called to teach God's Word, be on guard against a religious spirit operating through you that goes beyond teaching the Word to controlling and manipulating people into obeying Jesus. Share truth with integrity and allow the Holy Spirit to do the rest. In other words, you do your job, and He will do His.

Pastors and Discouragement Attack

There is a specific demonic attack that targets pastors and it's called discouragement. The truth is that discouragement can quickly turn into depression and even suicide if satan is successful. More pastors are killing themselves than at any other time in history because of this demonic attack.

Discouragement comes to steal our joy, fill us with hopelessness, and remove the desire to praise and worship.

Discouragement blurs our vision. If we don't confront depression, it eventually leads to unbelief, which is sin.

I heard the story that one day the devil was auctioning off his tools. They were highly priced—laziness, pride, hate, envy, and jealousy. One tool was not for sale. Someone asked, *"Why is that tool not for sale?"* Satan whispered, *"I can't afford to get rid of that one. It's my chief tool—discouragement! I can pry open any heart with that tool, and once I'm inside, I can do anything I want!"*

If we linger in discouragement it can be costly. Its sense of defeat and hopelessness saps us of energy and vision. It can consume a lot of time. It can keep us from doing what we need to do because we don't want to face it. And discouragement can even be contagious, weakening even other people's faith.

David asks the question in Psalm 42:11 (NLT):

Why am I discouraged? Why is my heart so sad? I will put my hope in God! I will praise him again—my Savior and my God!

Overcoming Discouragement Attack

There are three primary ways we can have victory over discouragement:

1. We strengthen ourselves in the Lord.

2. We focus on what God *is* doing, not on what we think He is *not* doing.

3. We are flexible and remain dedicated to the work He is calling us to do.

Whether you are a pastor growing in influence or know one, I encourage you to pray for pastors. They are constantly plagued and attacked by a demonic spirit of discouragement that wants to put them in depression and lead them to suicide.

Evangelists and Vanity Attack

In Luke 4:18 (NASB), Jesus gives the job description of an evangelist when He says, *"The Spirit of the Lord is upon Me, because He anointed Me to bring good news to the poor. He has sent Me to proclaim release to captives, and recovery of sight to the blind, to set free those who are oppressed."* In this one verse, we can recognize that evangelists are called to:

1. Preach good news to the poor

2. Proclaim the gospel to sinners

3. Operate in signs, wonders, and miracles

4. Cast demons out of people

When an evil spirit of vanity attacks evangelists, they stop fulfilling their God-given assignments in the earth and falsely believe that their calling is all about platforms, stages, and applause. By definition, the word *vanity* means "excessive pride in or admiration of one's own appearance and achievements." When a vanity attack has been successful against one of God's evangelists, they become consumed with the size of crowds, offerings, and more. This dangerous deception keeps them away from their real calling—the highways and byways where the lost can be found, the oppressed can be set free, and the prisons where the demonized can be delivered.

Overcoming Vanity Attack

Evangelists overcome this demonic attack by staying on assignment and not allowing the allurement of social media fame to entice them into sin and compromise. For evangelists, it's all about the harvest and souls. It is better to be famous in Heaven than on the earth. The gospel has never been about fame or future but rather the invitation to deny ourselves, pick up our cross and follow Jesus. Being content in the sphere of influence God has given you protects you from operating in vanity and delusion.

SPIRITUAL WARFARE OR NOT?

Spiritual warfare is real. Satan is actively attacking men and women of God with influence in order to distract and destroy them. Committing sin and facing the consequence for our words and actions is also real. When God brings correction to our lives and calls for repentance, we should not and cannot claim it's a demonic attack.

This is why I wrote chapter 4 of this book, "Healthy Community and Accountability." I understand by experience just how difficult it is to discern whether God is bringing correction or satan is attacking us in some seasons. People with influence must accept that they will constantly have the public weighing in on their decisions and words. The only way through all these opinions and discerning what you should listen to or not, is having trusting voices in our lives that can help us recognize whether we are being attacked by the enemy or if there is actually an area in our lives that needs to be confronted and addressed.

Years ago, I was being publicly slandered online. My character was being called into question, and it was very painful. I called a spiritual father of mine and said to him, "Have you read the false accusations about me online?" I was looking for some sympathy.

His response shocked me! He said, "What if they are right, Jeremiah? What if they are right?"

I responded in disbelief. How could my spiritual father even dare to ask me this question? His response forever changed my outlook on even demonic attack.

He said, "Jeremiah, God is so good that if we will allow Him, He can even use false accusation to develop more character and integrity inside us."

This was a very difficult lesson to learn, but I am so grateful for the guidance I was given during that season of my life.

As influencers, we do not have to listen to everyone, but we should be submitted and accountable to leaders who really know us and can help us operate with common sense and humility. No, not everything is a demon or spiritual warfare. There are many seasons in our lives when we just made a mistake, and will have to repent and accept the consequences. There are times when we must not blame the devil, but rather take responsibility for our actions and learn the lessons God wants us to learn.

WALKING IN THE FEAR OF THE LORD

P salm 25:14 (NASB) says, *"The secret of the Lord is for those who fear Him, and He will make them know His covenant."* Out of all the secrets that could be given regarding the price and power of influence, what it means to walk in the fear of the Lord is the greatest of them all! The fear of the Lord is the gift that empowers us to see the difference between God's assessment of us and our opinion of ourselves.

It is a very sobering reality to recognize that we could be growing in influence with people at the expense of becoming displeasing to God. As influencers, we are learning how to define success, not from people's applause and praise, but from the "Well done" by our heavenly Father. Pleasing Him and obeying His commands, no matter the cost, should always be our primary source of motivation to be successful.

Proverbs 14:26 (NASB) says, *"In the fear of the Lord, there is strong confidence...."* We gain confidence in the call that God has placed in our lives by learning how to fear Him. People who fear the Lord are not timid. They actually gain confidence in knowing who God is and what He says about them.

Psalm 2:11 (NLT) says, *"Serve the Lord with reverent fear, and rejoice with trembling."* Fearing God produces supernatural joy. We learn how to rejoice in the fact that He is God and we are not. What a relief!

Proverbs 19:23 (NLT) says, *"Fear of the Lord leads to life, bringing security and protection from harm."* Walking in the fear of the Lord releases peace and satisfaction to our souls. It protects us from evil and the plans of the enemy.

The book of Acts tells us there was astounding growth and multiplication in the early Church. What was the primary factor contributing to this phenomena? Acts 9:31 in the New King James version says, *"Then the churches throughout all Judea, Galilee, and Samaria had peace and were edified. And walking in the fear of the Lord and in the comfort of the Holy Spirit, they were multiplied."* Walking in the fear of the Lord produces a comfort that can only come from Him and multiplication as a result of His favor and blessing. If we desire increased influence, we should try the fear of the Lord!

JESUS WALKED INTO THE ROOM

I have been preaching and teaching on the fear of the Lord according to the Bible for many years. I am familiar with the passages and verses and have spent much time in prayer concerning them. However, it was not until I had a life-changing encounter with Jesus Christ that the reality of the fear of the Lord marked me in an experiential way.

I was on a 21-day fast in 2019 seeking God for direction in regard to my life and ministry. I had successfully planted churches, written books, traveled, and appeared on television, and now I was desiring clarity on what was next. I was in my bedroom sitting in my chair praying, when suddenly a man glowing in bright light and clothed in white walked into my room. I was stunned to say the least. He was as real to me as anyone I have ever met with in person.

I immediately knew it was not an angel—it was Jesus Christ. Human words fail to describe my encounter with Him. What I experienced was a simultaneous sensation of wanting to bow down as low before Him as I possibly could and, at the same time, wanting to run out of the room and get as far away as possible from Him as I could.

When Isaiah saw the Lord and said, *"Woe is me,"* that really is what it felt like. Fearing God is not being afraid of Him as if He is some kind of abuser to His kids; rather, it is acknowledging that He is holy and totally unlike us. He is worthy of all honor, respect, and worship.

As I stared into the eyes of Jesus, He truly was and is the most beautiful Man I have ever seen. The kindness in His eyes and yet the intensity of His facial features kept me unable to move or speak. It was as if time stood still for eternity. As I stood there in total fascination, completely aware of my own sin and failures and, at the same time, captivated by the wonder of the Son of Man, I experientially knew what the fear of the Lord is and feels like for the first time in my life.

Jesus Christ is truly so beautiful, so magnificent, so glorious, so beyond words that the only right response to being in His presence is worship and trembling before Him in awe and wonder. Psalm 33:8 (NASB) says, *"Let all the earth fear the Lord; let all the inhabitants of the world stand in awe of Him."*

INFLUENCE AND BOASTING

It is important for us to constantly admit that without the grace, strength, and support of God, we could not accomplish anything. Jesus said it plainly to His disciples, *"...apart from Me you can do nothing"* (John 15:5 NASB). Paul the apostle arrived at a startling conclusion toward the

THE FEAR OF THE LORD

is BEAUTY

that makes you tremble.

end of his life and ministry. He influenced his generation in extraordinary ways. He dared to acknowledge all of his accomplishments and human achievements, yet wrote and said they were like dung (garbage, rubbish) compared to knowing Jesus Christ! What strong language Paul used. He considered everything that he had accomplished like feces (human waste) when it came to how much he truly treasured Jesus Christ.

Could we as influencers in this generation compile a list of all that we have achieved and accomplished—the awards, material possessions, lives impacted by the gospel, notoriety, and more—and with confidence declare to all our fans and followers that it means absolutely nothing compared to an intimate relationship with Jesus Christ?

The truth is that the more we boast in our own success, the more it reveals how much we truly do not know Jesus Christ. We may teach and share knowledge about Him, but truly encountering Him in His Word and in His presence will never leave us the same.

A.W. Tozer said, "When we come into relationship with Jesus, we start to learn astonished reverence, breathless adoration, awesome fascination, and lofty admiration of who God is. I believe the reverential fear of God mixed with love, fascination, astonishment, admiration, and devotion is the most enjoyable state and the most purifying emotion the human soul can know."[1]

DON'T BURY YOUR TALENTS

We live in a time when there are so many unhealthy extremes when it comes to the price and power of influence. One extreme has the constant self-promoters who operate in pride and arrogance. I have addressed this attitude and falsehood over and over again throughout this book. May we walk in humility, purity, and the fear of the Lord.

The opposite extreme of self-promotion is when people God has called to influence their generation bury their talents. These individuals are so afraid of boasting in themselves that by keeping silent they don't realize they are failing to boast in God. I do not believe God takes issue with us sharing with others about what we have accomplished. His issue is regarding to whom we give the credit and glory.

Paul told the Corinthians, *"I have worked harder than all of the apostles...."* What a potentially arrogant and prideful statement! However, he finished his statement by declaring how he worked harder than everyone by saying, *"though it was not I, but the grace of God [His unmerited favor and blessing which was] with me"* (1 Corinthians 15:10 AMP). Paul's boast was in the Lord, but he never shrank back from sharing all that he had accomplished.

Whether we are guilty of self-promoting or burying our talents, we must remember that to fear the Lord is to obey

Him and follow His voice at all costs. Walking in the fear of the Lord for many is going to look like overcoming our insecurities and all our excuses for why we are not qualified for influence—and start speaking up. Talking too much when God is saying to remain silent and not talking at all when God is asking us to speak up are both sinful and we need to repent.

Psalm 25:12 (NLT) says, *"Who are those who fear the Lord? He will show them the path they should choose."* God is extending a clear invitation to influencers. He wants to teach us His ways, but we must fear Him. Jesus desires to encounter our hearts. He is looking for men and women who want to make Him famous in their generation. Will we accept whatever influence God wants to give us, small or large and walk in humility? When we are under spiritual warfare attack or facing the jealousy of others, will we choose forgiveness and not allow our hearts to grow bitter and offended?

When Jesus Christ cried out, *"It is finished,"* He opened the door for the Holy Spirit to declare over humanity, "I'm just getting started." Today, tomorrow, and forever, may a generation of influencers partner with the indwelling work of the Holy Spirit to lead and guide us into all truth. Amen!

NOTE

1.   A. W. Tozer, *Whatever Happened to Worship?* (Camp Hill, PA: Christian Publications, 1985).

ABOUT
JEREMIAH JOHNSON

Jeremiah Johnson entered into full-time ministry in 2009 after graduating from Southeastern University with a Bachelor's degree in theology and a minor in missions.

Over the past 15 years, God called Jeremiah to successfully plant churches in Florida (Heart of the Father Ministry) and North Carolina (The Ark Fellowship). Operating in a strong apostolic capacity, Jeremiah builds and disciples elder teams and fivefold ministry leaders who are graced to function in the local church with love and care.

Along with planting and establishing local churches in an apostolic capacity, Jeremiah has also had the privilege of ministering prophetically in 43 states and 27 foreign nations. He typically ministers in 40-50 churches and conferences every year. Oftentimes receiving dreams and visions for leaders and regions, Jeremiah has been used mightily to further the work of God in many different areas of the USA and the world.

With years of apostolic experience in the local church as well as traveling and ministering prophetically abroad, Jeremiah has also invested much of his time into authoring 15 books and being a popular television guest on the *700 Club, Daystar, TBN,* Sid Roth's *It's Supernatural,* and *GodTV.* He enjoys writing and sharing about his experiences including church planting, the fivefold ministry, and various encounters he has had with God.

The Johnsons currently lead an equipping center in Kannapolis, North Carolina, called The Altar Global, which exists to equip and train a generation for the work of ministry. They specialize in: equipping everyday believers through their one-year discipleship program; training prophets and prophetic people in mentorships with Jeremiah; impacting the next generation through Camp Goshen; and investing in church leaders through the fivefold family network. For more information, please visit: thealtarglobal.com or jeremiahjohnson.tv.

YOUR Prophetic COMMUNITY

Sign up for a **FREE** subscription to the Destiny Image digital magazine and get awesome content delivered directly to your inbox!

destinyimage.com/signup

Sign up for Cutting-Edge Messages that Supernaturally Empower You

- Gain valuable insights and guidance based on biblical principles
- Deepen your faith and understanding of God's plan for your life
- Receive regular updates and prophetic messages
- Connect with a community of believers who share your values and beliefs

Experience Fresh Video Content that Reveals Your Prophetic Inheritance

- Receive prophetic messages and insights
- Connect with a powerful tool for spiritual growth and development
- Stay connected and inspired on your faith journey

Listen to Powerful Podcasts that Propel You into God's Presence Every Day

- Deepen your understanding of God's prophetic assignment
- Experience God's revival power throughout your day
- Learn how to grow spiritually in your walk with God

In the Right Hands, This Book Will Change Lives!

Most of the people who need this message will not be looking for this book. To change their lives, you need to **put a copy of this book in their hands.**

Our ministry is constantly seeking methods to find the people who need this anointed message to change their lives. **Will you help us reach these people?**

Extend this ministry by sowing three, five, ten, or *even more* books today and change people's lives for the better! Your generosity will be part of catalyzing the Great Awakening that many have been prophesying and praying for.

From
Jeremiah Johnson

Are we prepared for the glory and the cleansing to come?

The Bible promises that judgment begins in the house of God. Many people avoid this intense passage in fear of the word "judgment." As New Covenant believers, we can take comfort that this judgment brings life through a healthy fear of the Lord. Instead of warnings of hellfire and condemnation, this judgment brings a cleansing that will set the stage for the greatest outpouring of glory, prophetic thunder, and supernatural power the world has ever seen.

God is simply looking for a people made ready—a house that is compatible with the glory He wants to fill it with!

Jeremiah Johnson is a church planter, pioneer of Maranatha Ministry School, bestselling author and globally recognized prophet. In *Judgment on the House of God*, Jeremiah presents an impassioned prophetic word that challenges Christians to live without impurity and compromise, not through the bondage of legalism, but through ignited, burning hearts of passion towards the Lord.

A great and wonderful outpouring is coming. Now is the time to set things in order so that you can be a pure vessel that the power and presence of God can flow through!

Purchase your copy wherever books are sold

From
Jeremiah Johnson

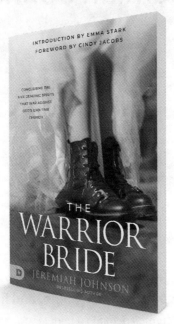

These Five Insidious Spirits Have Marked You For Destruction

Does it feel as if the host of hell is aimed at preventing you from advancing, from stepping into God's destiny for your life?

They are — and their attacks are planned, plotted, and targeted by five insidious spirits hell-bent on destroying the body of Christ: Leviathan, Jezebel, Religious Spirit, Depression, and Vanity. Deployed to war against the five-fold ministry offices — apostles, prophets, teachers, pastors, and evangelists — these demonic agents coordinate their attacks not just against leaders, but also against every believer who occupies these functions in any sphere of influence.

With passion and piercing insights, international prophet and bestselling author Jeremiah Johnson exposes these demonic forces and their tactics, empowering you with courage to prevail against any attack by operating as Jesus' end-time church — *the Warrior Bride*.

Now it's your turn to live on the offense, crushing the enemy's assaults every time they come against you!

Purchase your copy wherever books are sold

From

Jeremiah Johnson

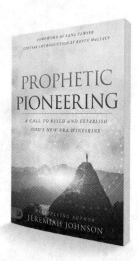

A world plagued with darkness is waiting for a prophetic people to arise, shine, and light the way!

Days of crisis and turmoil demand a people who are plugged into Heaven's activity. Old operating systems that built empires in the name of Christianity, but created shallow, compromising disciples, are crumbling under the weight of global instability.

In the midst of a season of great personal challenge and persecution, author, church leader, and prophet Jeremiah Johnson received fresh blueprints and new prophetic strategies on how to navigate the days of challenge and opportunity ahead.

Prophetic Pioneering is a call for you to be part of the radical Jesus People remnant that is arising in this critical hour! This invitation is not exclusive to pastors and ministry leaders; the call to see the coming move of God and build in accordance with the activity of Heaven, is just as relevant in the marketplace as it to the minister.

The hour is urgent, dark, and late... but the opportunity to be carriers of prophetic solutions has never been greater. **Will you take your place as a prophetic pioneer?**

Purchase your copy wherever books are sold

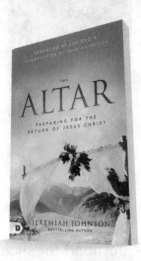

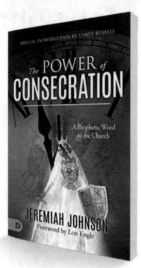